because I am a Girl

EBURY PRESS

An imprint of Penguin Random House

EBURY PRESS

USA | Canada | UK | Ireland | Australia
New Zealand | India | South Africa | China | Singapore

Ebury Press is part of the Penguin Random House group of companies whose addresses can be found at global.penguinrandomhouse.com

Published by Penguin Random House India Pvt. Ltd
4th Floor, Capital Tower 1, MG Road,
Gurugram 122 002, Haryana, India

Penguin Random House India

First published by Random House India 2012

10 9 8 7 6 5 4 3 2

ISBN 9788184001563

For sale in the Indian Subcontinent only

Typeset in Palatino Linotype by Jojy Philip
Printed at Manipal Technologies Limited, India

www.penguin.co.in

FSC www.fsc.org MIX Paper from responsible sources FSC® C043100

This is a legitimate digitally printed version of the book and therefore might not have certain extra finishing on the cover.

Contents

Introduction

Perhaps there is no greater sense of triumph than the one achieved by a disadvantaged individual through an intense struggle for her dignity and livelihood against a hostile social and economic background.

The realization dawned on me as I got progressively involved, six years ago, with the work being done by Plan India with disadvantaged children and their communities on various aspects of their lives.

Plan India has programmes that focus on issues related to the girl child. And *Because I Am a Girl* is one of its major initiatives. In the process of implementing *Because I Am a Girl* across several states of the country, the Plan India teams came across many inspiring stories of courageous young girls who challenged their circumstances and through sheer determination and unrelenting effort, rose above them. This book presents a selection of seven such stimulating stories.

Each story in this collection is not simply a journalistic report of a sequence of events in a particular girl's life; it is an attempt to gain an insight into their long and sustained struggles to negotiate the difficult conditions in order to be able to achieve a robust sense of self, inner pride, and restore a modicum of dignity.

These are the stories of young girls who make a conscious decision to take the risk and initiate the effort to change the claustrophobic situation of their current lives, to break free of the shackles of tradition and taboos that restrain their natural growth, to push open the doors of their dark rooms, to emerge in the sunlight to claim the freedom and opportunity which is rightfully theirs. The outcome in each case is positive and even uplifting but always tempered with humility, hope, and resilience. One important milestone in almost all the stories though is a stage in the journey when the struggling protagonist comes in contact with an initiative of Plan India and the positive turn her struggle takes thereafter. These are the stories of empowerment through right knowledge and guidance provided by Plan India through its various outreach programmes.

Seven young women from different walks of life were invited for a one-on-one meeting with the girls and write about the experience of their interaction in their very own words. In the subtly unfolding *Walking the Line*, Anjum Hasan, through her protagonist Mina, discovers a community near Bharatpur, Rajasthan, where parents customarily send their young daughters to join the 'line' to support the family. As Mina's husband Mahendar says, 'I know boys around here who live off their sisters' earnings and wear gold chains this thick... Cielo, Mercedes, you name it, they have it.' Mina is one such daughter who decides to leave the line when she meets Mahendar. But before that she has lived years through the 'line'. Now, free from the compulsion to sell her body, but having to work hard with her husband to earn a living, she is asked 'Are you finally happy, Mina?' 'Of course,' says Mina quickly before her emotions can slip through. 'Anyone who leaves the line can only be happy.'

Shahana Goswami (*Walk of Life*) picks up a conversation with a young girl (not so young as she soon discovers) in a Mumbai local train. Intrigued and fascinated to know more about the person, Shahana accompanies the girl to her small home in a slum where they 'are the only Hindu family' in the neighbourhood. It is a fascinating encounter during which a young girl's tough life opens up like a book and the writer is able to browse through some random pages. It is only when the writer gets up to leave and turns back to her saying, 'Arrey, I forgot to ask you...' 'Sunita,' she corrected and laughed out loud. And it is while telling her story that the girl discovers pride in who she is, her sense of self as she declares her name, her pride layered over by her laughter.

Another meeting, another story. Meenakshi Madhavan Reddy (*Any Other Sort of Teenager*) meets a tall, shy girl named Radha in a lunch home in Hyderabad, making us enter the world of migrant workers in a big city. Daughter of landless parents, now earning their livelihood as migrant labourers in Hyderabad, Radha manages to get a 'proper' office job, with a computer and a cell phone to herself. And that's precisely what invites the jibes from jobless boys hanging around at street corners in her neighborhood. 'Oho, Miss Office, think you're so big!' Of whatever she earns, one half is saved for her brother's college tuition fee while the other half is set aside for her dowry. Her mother is obsessed with marrying her off to Ram Mama, her uncle, but Radha's ambition is to become a nurse. Will she ever? One hopes one day she will. In the meanwhile, having negotiated tough times, she has grown confident enough to say no to the marriage. Henceforth she decides to take her own decisions about her life.

Pooja Bedi (*Born to Die*), disturbed and enraged by the news of female infanticide in Devra, a village in Rajasthan with an alarming female population of only 13, all below the age of ten years, contacts Plan India. She is taken to Uttar Pradesh to meet Pushpa, a woman '...who had been subjected to brutal humiliation by her husband for bearing a third girl child.' On this journey with Pooja, we discover a family that defies all our perceptions of a traditional and conservative middle class North Indian patriarchal family. Ramrati, a 61-year-old, uneducated mother-in-law of Pushpa, presides over a family that is surprisingly progressive, liberal and sensitive towards the girls. It is perhaps her understanding and support that has shielded Pushpa against her husband's escalating brutality. But the story does not end there. How can Pushpa be sure that she will not be forced to bear a child again by her son-obsessed husband? Empowered by the support of her mother-in-law and the younger women of the family, a quiet Pushpa is determined not to bear another child in the overreaching quest for a son. 'If he so desperately wants a boy, we can adopt one and give an orphan a good life.'

The name of the protagonist of Aditi Rao's '*The Thousand-piece Jigsaw*' is Naazma, which literally means 'the one who looks after'. Naazma is a little angel. Even when little, she is seen content and smiling and looking after some creature or the other, picking up puppies, feeding them, finding homes for kittens, scattering seeds for birds, and rocking wailing babies to sleep. But even angels like Naazma have to face a harsh life. The daughter of a migrant worker from Hyderabad working in a factory in Mumbai, Naazma's too is a tough journey but her strength is her compassion and indefatigable spirit. One day she will surely become the nurse that she dreams of becoming..

In Namrita Bachchan's evocatively narrated '*A Mandi Life*', this is how we first see its protagonist, Puja, who 'lay squashed between her two sweating sisters under their mother's sagging bed in the improvised shack they called home. She was trying to breathe'. Living in such claustrophobic conditions, Puja is determined to learn English and fulfill her dream of becoming a soldier. By the time we read the last line of her brave passage through life in the vegetable market, Mandi, we realize that not only will this little girl learn English but she also has it in her to become a soldier as well.

Gul Afshaan is from Assam. After the raging Brahamputra washes away her home and everything else with it, leaving her family homeless and destitute, Gul Afshaan and her parents relocate to Delhi, thanks to the kindness of her uncle who lives in the city. When Nafisa Ali Sodhi (*Dignity*) meets

Gul Afshaan, the 13-year-old girl is living a hard life; she studies in a school and also works as a rag-picker before and after school hours. 'These days I go to the station only at four o'clock in the morning and am back by 6:30 am as I have to go to school. Papa earns two thousand rupees a month. He picks garbage in a push cart going from one colony to another. And I manage to make a hundred rupees on a good day.' It's a tough life for such a young girl, but even when given a chance, Gul Afshaan would choose not to return to her village in Assam, 'I would like to stay here now. I know this place.'

The stories of these seven girls are lives in progress. But the one element that is common to the dreams of all these girls is the absence of selfishness. Their foremost concern is to bring comfort and dignity to the lives of their parents, particularly the mother, and their siblings, their own well-being always coming second. In the face of the most challenging of circumstances, these young girls shield themselves and their families with compassion and care and, of course, boundless hope.

Govind Nihalani
November 7, 2011

Nirma

(Polio-afflicted young girl of about 18-20 years from Bajju block in western Rajasthan)

When I first attended the Balika Shivir I couldn't read or write. It was there that I became familiar with letters and started making sense of them. I stayed there for about six months and slowly made an effort to start reading books. I was thrilled by my achievement. In fact, all of us—the girls who had come to the camp—were illiterate and we were away from our families. But as we spent time at the camp and started reading and writing, our joy knew no bounds. For me, however, the happiness had multiple facets as I had not only started reading but I was also learning how to walk on my own at the camp. It was all very special!

Walking the Line

Anjum Hasan

Mina is standing barefoot in a faded nightie at the counter of her little shop, selling small packets of homemade gur sweets, sachets of shampoo and washing powder, and bottles of soft drinks to the children who come up to the shop with coins clutched in their sweaty fists. She's also selling hot samosas at ₹4 a piece, wrapped in squares of old newspaper. Her husband, Mahendar, is frying the samosas on a kerosene stove in an adjoining room.

'They're not perfect today,' he says. 'The crust should be a little softer, more chewy.'

Sitting on the floor of the shop in a T-shirt and jeans, the couple's 11-year-old daughter, Abhilasha, is cutting the dough left over from the samosas into fat strips, which Mahendar will later fry into namkeen. Every time she notices me looking at her, she flicks back her long, shiny hair, smiles to herself, and continues her namkeen cutting with renewed seriousness. No one bothers to swat away the flies that work diligently on every surface in still, black droves. Mahendar has one ear on the TV playing in the inner room. A crucial India–Australia cricket match is on. As soon as there's a power cut, which is about every fifteen minutes, he switches on the battery-operated transistor standing near the stove. On his forearm, a tattooed word has been inked over, and the word 'Mina' tattooed next to it.

Mina ignores the cricket. From time to time, she steps away from the counter and leans against the doorjamb separating the two rooms to continue with the story she's telling me.

Before she married Mahendar seven years ago, Mina used to be a bar dancer in Mumbai. In 2005, the family returned to this village in Rajasthan's Bharatpur district to set up life in the very place from which Mina had made her journey outward, following the compulsions of her trade as a sex worker. Mina belongs to the once-nomadic Bedia community—scattered over Rajasthan, Madhya Pradesh, and Uttar Pradesh—whose men are known to sell their sisters and daughters into prostitution.

At one point, after a customer has called her out and she's returned, I say to Mina, the thread of our earlier conversation having been broken, 'Tell me something nice that you remember about your life in Mumbai.'

'I don't remember anything, I've forgotten everything,' says Mina, smiling.

She has small, shiny teeth and the kajal glistening in her eyes is the only make-up she's wearing. She could be an elder sister to Abhilasha. Mina speaks slowly and at the end of every second sentence, she drawls a slow 'Haan (Yes),' for emphasis and gives a charming little shake of her neck.

'How many years did you spend in Mumbai?'

'Two.'

'And how did you meet Mahendar?'

'He was working there, as a manager in the dance bar. Haan.'

As it turns out, Mina remembers a great deal—both about Mumbai and about her life in the village as the daughter of a man who tried and failed to do a little farming to make ends meet. Her mother, she says, only managed to serve them one meal a day of coarse chappatis and chutney. Mina's four brothers, illiterate like their parents, would earn ₹100 to ₹150 a day, washing plates at dhabas. From there they graduated to breaking stones for a living. For some time they grazed goats. Mina remembers trying to stay awake through winter nights as a 12-year-old. Her father would make a fire out of a few sticks, and he, along with Mina and her two sisters, would camp by the Agra–Jaipur highway, hoping to hook a customer—anyone willing to pay for half an hour with any of the girls. She remembers how there was a time when she was servicing up to fifteen trucker clients a day in one of the little concrete huts off the road,

Prostitution

According to Human Rights Watch, there are approximately 15 million prostitutes in India. There are more than 100,000 women in prostitution in Mumbai, Asia's largest sex industry centre. Girls in prostitution in India, Pakistan, and the Middle East are tortured, held in virtual imprisonment, sexually abused, and raped. India, along with Thailand and the Philippines, has 1.3 million children in its sex-trade centres. India and Pakistan are the main destinations for children under sixteen who are trafficked in South Asia.

About 60 percent of those trafficked into prostitution are adolescent girls in the age group of 12 to 16 years. These figures are corroborated by a study done by the Department of Women and Children in thirteen sensitive districts of Uttar Pradesh. It shows that in a sample of 1,341 sex workers, brothel-based prostitution accounted for 793 and family-based prostitution came close at 548.

screened by bushes, which her father and brothers built once the business got going. She remembers playing marbles as a 15-year-old, oblivious to the fact that she was pregnant with Abhilasha.

As Mina tells me all this, standing before me, playing with the beads of her mangalsutra (wedding necklace), I wait to detect a note of bitterness or rage.

'My father used to lie in a drunken stupor all day,' says Mina matter-of-factly. 'My sisters look after him now.'

Mina's elder sisters, who stayed back in the village, have built a house where their three brothers and their wives and children live, along with their father. They also take care of the youngest brother who isn't married yet.

'What does he do?'

'Nothing,' says Mina, in a tone that suggests—obviously nothing. 'We used to try to send him to school but he ran back every time. We'd beat him and send him back and then he'd run away again so we let him be. Haan,' she says then, smiling her attractive smile, extending the plate of just-fried samosas that Mahendar has handed her. 'Here, have a samosa.'

'And your mother?'

'Woh toh off ho gayi (she got off),' says Mina, momentarily distracted by a car advertisement on TV. 'She broke her leg and became very weak; I gave her a bottle of blood, so did my elder brother. But then she just stopped eating and drinking.'

'Did she come to visit you when you lived in Mumbai?'

'Of course, lots of times.'

'Did she ever feel bad about what she and your father had to make you do?'

'Everyone knows the pain involved. But what's the point of feeling bad? Majboori thi (it was necessary),' says Mina. She grows thoughtful for a minute, then adds, 'If she'd asked me, I'd have answered back because I was earning. I'd have said—why didn't you ask me before? Ab toh jaisa kat raha hai waisa kat raha hai.'

'So you never spoke about it with your parents?' I persist.

'We were poor,' explains Mina patiently. 'We didn't have enough to eat. What can people do in these villages? They can either make hooch from gur or send their girls into the trade.'

'I've been speaking to a few other women and they say that things are changing, that they will never send their own girls into this line,' I say.

'That's what they say...' says Mahendar gruffly, who's been listening to us silently for a while, '... because they have a little money in their hands. As soon as the money goes, what option will they have left? It's not like these women are married. It's not like they're running a business from which they'll keep raising profits.'

'They really want to educate their girls, they want to send them out of the village to study,' I say.

'Mina used to go to school. Did that make a difference?' asks Mahendar.

Mina studied till Class 4 in a government school before her work put an end to her studies. 'I didn't learn any English,' she says regretfully. 'In those days they introduced ABC only in the sixth.' In the last few years, helping Abhilasha with her school work, Mina has picked up enough, she proudly tells me, to be able to teach up to Class 5 students if she ever needs to.

There's a subdued excitement in her when she talks about Abhilasha's studies, which I notice a clear echo of in Mahendar's voice. He has got it all worked out. He plans to help Abhilasha clear the entrance exams for the prestigious residential school—the Jawahar Navodaya Vidyalaya. After that, he wants her to take a BA in history, geography, and political science. He'll send her to Jaipur for coaching in the last year of her BA so that she can prepare for her Civil Services exam. Mahendar wants Abhilasha to return to Bharatpur district as a Collector.

'Of course, only if she has the aptitude for it,' he says after he has laid out this elaborate plan. Abhilasha calmly hands over the platter of cut namkeen to Mahendar. We could be discussing someone she has never heard of. Abhilasha was raised by her grandmother till she was four. When Mina and Mahendar married, they brought her to Mumbai. Now she goes to the school run by a local NGO.

'What do you think of this plan, Abhilasha?' I ask her.

'We'll see,' she says, giggling, and starts to unpack a carton of biscuits that her father has bought for the shop.

Mahendar is done with his samosa frying and is finishing up the namkeen.

'Delicious samosa,' I say, mopping up the last bits with the tangy saunth and the pudina chutney that Abhilasha gave me in small glass bowls.

'Not the best,' says Mahendar. 'The dough should have been a little looser. You should try my lassi some time; I make the best lassi in the world. And Mina didn't even know how to set good dahi. I taught her how to make dahi so thick you can cut it with a knife, like barfi, and as sweet as barfi too. Not sour at all.'

Mahendar was born into the Yadav caste in Patiala, in a landed family that was related to the Nawab's. His brother is a magistrate. One uncle was a colonel in the army; another an official in the telephone department, a very upright man who never took a bribe in his life. 'Sahi ko tang nahi kiya, galat ko chora nahi (never bothered a good person, never let a bad one go),' he says pithily of this relative.

Early in life, Mahendar took some tough decisions. He decided that he would not depend financially on his family for any longer than he strictly needed to. He also decided that the woman he'd marry would be someone he had rescued from 'the line', an ambition of which even God might approve. 'Bhagwan bhi bolein, waah kya kaam kiya hai. If I'd chosen to have an arranged marriage within my community that would have meant ₹5 lakh and a Maruti car for me,' says Mahendar, smirking.

Mahendar privately took a BA in history and then worked in a string of businesses before ending up as the manager of a dance bar in Thane on a salary of ₹30,000 a month. I ask him where he learnt to cook. 'I learnt by watching,' he says. 'My family had a mithai shop and I would watch. I never actually made the sweets myself,' he insists. 'I just watched.'

Mahendar is at pains to establish that he is not what he appears to be—a vest-wearing halwai, grimy with sweat, frying samosas for a living. But neither does he tell me the story of his life in a straightforwardly chronological way. He starts enthusiastically on things, then veers off if I ask too many questions. When I show him my recorder and ask if I can switch it on, he's very clear that I cannot.

'No recording and no photographs,' he says. 'They'll recognize my voice and my face.'

'Who are they?'

'People in Gurgaon, Delhi...they all know me,' he says vaguely.

He jumps from talking about learning how to make sweets to telling me about the time he decided to spread awareness about HIV among sex workers and landed up in Alwar district with bags full of free condoms. He was arrested for suspicious behaviour.

'Alwar is where you should go,' says Mahendar repeatedly.

He insists that I am in the wrong place if it is the exploitation of women I'm concerned about. Alwar is the district in Rajasthan that made national headlines in the summer of 2010 for a prostitution racket that thrived on the basis of injecting young girls with a veterinary drug called Oxytocin. Normally used to induce lactation in cows and buffaloes, injecting Oxytocin into 6- and 7-year-old girls caused them to reach puberty abnormally early and start looking like young women, ripe for what is known as the 'flesh trade'.

Mahendar and Mina know Alwar. When she informed her parents that she was leaving the line and had found someone who wanted to marry her, they beat her and packed her off to Alwar. Mahendar traced her there, took her to Mumbai, and married her.

Mahendar's famous samosas have now run out and Mina laughs as she turns away the youths who come to buy more. She waters her plants—roses and marigolds in two pots on the wall—the small, lush flowers an incredible sight in this dusty village of open drains and lanes smeared with dirt and dung. A small boy appears, wailing, a sharp stone in his raised fist, poised to strike at the head of an even smaller child who is fleeing from him, squealing. Mina chides the children gently and the stone is eventually dropped. Mahendar is lamenting something in the cricket game. Glancing into the small, dark, inner room, I see melted gur glistening in plastic bags, lined up on the floor.

'What's the gur for?' I ask no one in particular.

'It's to make sweets with,' says Mahendar while, simultaneously, Mina says, 'It's to make hooch with.' I decide to change the subject.

'I've met women who've been in the line and left but none of them have married. They either can't find a man to marry them or they don't want to,' I say to Mahendar. 'You and Mina are a rarity.'

'How much do you think Australia will make? They're batting like devils,' says Mahendar.

After he's stepped in to check the score, he tells me, 'Only 5 percent of all men can be trusted.' During his time as manager of the dance bar, run by one Shetty from Karnataka, Mahendar says that the men were nothing but trouble, both the paisewale men and the taporis (hooligans): men who wanted to touch the girls, who got into fights, who got drunk and refused to leave. Also, he has seen scores of men marry bar dancers with the promise of rescuing them, only to send them back into the line and live off their earnings. 'My advice to the girls would always be, first live with the man for a year and observe his behaviour.'

After Mahendar and Mina got married, they ran a general store for a year in Chembur. It was doing well till the Mumbai floods of 2005 when Mahendar was marooned in the shop for two days and had to wade through chest-high water to get out. The water destroyed their goods. He never went back. They packed up and came to this village, not the one that Mina grew up in but close enough. I am curious to know what the village made of him.

'They all come to my shop. I stock Dove soap, I have sanitary pads. None of the other shops have these things.'

'Everyone treats us with respect,' says Mina. 'How can they not? People have become crorepatis sending their girls into this line. Don't be fooled by the appearance of this village, there are some very rich people here.'

'I know boys around here who live off their sisters' earnings and wear gold chains this thick,' adds Mahendar. 'Cielo, Mercedes, you name it, they have it.'

Mina and I are bumping along in a hired Bolero, going to meet her sisters, Shilpa and Shalini. She is telling me about her time in the Mira Road dance bar; she speaks of the bar dancers—as if unselfconsciously distancing herself from them—in the third person. They lived in an apartment building whose other residents had no clue about what the girls did for a living. They would dress in full-sleeved kurtas, their faces free of make-up, shoulder bags stuffed with their gear, and head out to the bar in the evening. To anyone who asked, they said they worked the night shift in a hospital.

'No one cares in Mumbai,' says Mina. 'People there don't make distinctions based on your caste or background.' Then, perking up to a loud, clicking sound coming from the one of the houses we're passing, she says, 'Atte ki chakki. There's no sound like the sound of a chakki.'

Later we see some women feeding plants into a manually operated fodder-threshing machine and I ask our driver, Anil, to stop so we can take a better look at it. The women come up to jeep, laughing, and I tell them I've never seen a machine like that before.

'Well, take a look at it now,' they say, amused.

'We're going to my sisters' village,' Mina tells them and they wave as we move away.

As the Bolero negotiates the narrow village lanes, I read signs promoting education painted in blue letters on whitewashed walls: 'Pehle dein shiksha daan, phir karein kanya daan (First provide education to your girl and only after that hand her over for marriage)' and 'Hum baccho ka ek hi nara, bhaymukt ho school hamara. (We, the children, have one slogan, face of fear be our school.)'

On the radio, a man is dispensing advice to mothers in a fatherly voice. 'Roast a little wheat flour in ghee, boil it with water or milk, add some sugar, and feed it to the infant. Also feed your child a boiled mash of whatever vegetable is in season.' I try to remember the statistics for child malnutrition in India. Do we have the worst record in the world or the second worst?

Soon we're out of the village and driving past fields of ripened wheat. There is also arhar dal and kala channa—crops which require very little water. It's harvest time for the kala channa. A woman riding pillion on a bike before us keeps picking the tender green pods off the stalks she's holding and popping them into her mouth. Anil laughs. 'By the time they get home, there'll be nothing left on those stalks.'

Lorries rumble towards us carrying huge slabs of the red stone this area is famous for—the same stone that Akbar had the nearby Fatehpur Sikri built from.

'Do you think this will end? Will families ever stop sending their daughters into the line?' I ask Mina.

'Earlier, people had very little sense,' says Mina. 'They thought that all that mattered was being fed. If you had food to eat, however you got it, you were fine. It's only now that people think about the future.'

'What do you see when you think of your future?'

'All I want is that Abhilasha should study and get a job, even if it's a ₹5000 a month job. I've told my brothers as well—educate your children and save for the future. Things are going to get very expensive. And there's trouble in this line too. They're closing down the dance bars in Mumbai, and there's some lafra happening in Delhi too. And the huts where my sisters used to see their clients... the panchayat has had most of them broken down and they haven't even got compensation.'

In recent years, the panchayat has been trying to erase this village's association with 'the line'.

According to a panchayat ruling, families were free to send their girls to the cities, but they could not operate inside the village. Those who, like Mina's sisters, didn't agree with the panchayat were exiled to the outskirts of the village but the harassment, says Mina, continues.

It's nightfall by the time we reach Shilpa and Shalini's home. As the Bolero swings down the sandy path, we see an old man, possibly Mina's father, on a charpoy outside. He's been woken from a nap and is glaring at the car. Mina ignores him completely and goes into the house, calling out for her sisters.

The house, built by those who have always lived in cramped environments, is clearly playing out the fantasy of space. One first enters a large corridor, half-open on one side, which serves no obvious purpose except to announce itself as a luxuriant emptiness. It is filled with a melee of children, like a kindergarten gone berserk. Mina strides into one of the three rooms strung along this corridor.

Shilpa, a tall, fair, buxom woman, joins us. Her elder daughter, Priya, has just finished Class 8 in the village school and she will have to go to the city if she is to study ahead. Shilpa is anxious.

'I don't want to send her to the city,' says Shilpa to Mina and Mina says, 'The city boys will put her in the bazaar, haan.'

Girls from communities like the Bedias, that are known to send their daughters into the line, are reviled. Boys will mock Priya for being a Bedia, and call her names. Shilpa describes the trouble she's recently had educating Priya. After an accident in Sawai Madhopur district in March 2010, when a bus packed with students and teachers collided with a jugaad—a makeshift truck—and plunged off a bridge, killing twenty-eight people, jugaads were banned in the state. For children like Priya, who had to walk a long distance to get a bus to school and were dependant on the jugaad, this was a blow. Shilpa says she's been anxious about Priya returning home from school in the darkness of early winter evenings.

'Where's Shalini?' I ask, about their eldest sister.

'Oh, she's around,' says Shilpa.

She says she's considering sending Priya to Jhunjhunu, 250 kilometres away, where there is a good residential school. No one in Jhunjhunu will know about Priya's antecedents. Echoing Mina, Shilpa says that the only thing that matters to her now is educating her daughter and seeing to it that she gets a good job.

'And then she'll marry?' I ask.

'If she finds a good man. Out of hundred men, ninety are crooks,' says Shilpa.

I watch the sisters talk, the camaraderie between them. Children go in and out of the room, fiddling with the television controls, finishing bottles of soft drinks and depositing them proudly on the table before us, clamouring to be held by Shilpa. Most of the children belong to the three brothers, who, with their wives, live in their own set of rooms at the back of the house. Each has eight or nine children. Their wives, the 'bahus', come in with their heads covered to be introduced to me. They are small, emaciated, shy-looking women with none of the easy confidence that Mina and Shilpa have. (The wives of Bedia men, unlike their sisters or mothers, are rarely sent into prostitution). The bahus mumble namastes and then drag their children away from the TV. Hung high on one wall of the room is a pristine pink teddy bear in a see-through plastic bag, way out of the reach of any of the kids. On another wall hangs a laminated blow-up of a strikingly beautiful, long-haired, jeans-clad girl, sprawled languidly against some cushions.

The sisters are talking about marriage. Shilpa is telling Mina the story of a village girl who was married off, and then went to visit a bar-dancer cousin in Mumbai. Seeing her cousin wearing make-up and nice clothes and going out to restaurants regularly, the girl returned with the idea that she wasn't interested in the husband any more. She was adamant about going into the line. The marriage had to be annulled and the money that the groom's family had spent on the wedding returned to them by the girl's family. Mina sighs and rolls her eyes at me, her expression saying—see, there are girls like this too. As for Mina, her heart was never in the line. She hated it from the beginning, which doesn't mean that she didn't put on her high heels and dance all night—'akhi akhi raat'—even when she had fever or had hurt her foot. It doesn't mean that she scrimped on sending money to her brothers and parents, and clothes for her sisters-in-laws, nephews, and nieces.

Shalini comes in finally, scrubbed and glowing. It turns out that she's been with a client in one of the huts they have out in front. She's just washed her face free of the make-up she had put on for him. Unlike Mina, both Shalini and Shilpa have remained in the village but they don't 'sit in the bazaar' any more. They have old customers who return to them, most of them out-of-towners from Agra and Jaipur. It was one such man that Shalini was with, a tourist who is a regular visitor to the Bharatpur bird sanctuary nearby.

'That's my daughter, Aditi,' says Shalini, pointing to the photograph on the wall. 'And this,' she says, lifting up a snotty, wild-haired toddler, 'is *her* daughter. She has two more.'

'You'd never guess Aditi's a mother of three,' says Mina. 'She's kept her figure.'

Aditi was a bar dancer who now acts in television serials in Mumbai and drives a scooter. She speaks English and is as fair as a foreigner, according to her mother and aunts. When she visited a few weeks ago, all the other kids thought she was a tourist and ran after her, asking for toffees. There are photographs of her in the other rooms too; she is clearly the family hero, the girl who turned her disadvantage on its head.

I am starting to appreciate the tricky calculus of relationships that Mina and her sisters have to negotiate. Mina has had the immeasurable good luck of finding a man willing to marry her despite her background. And a good man at that—one who not only doesn't beat her, but doesn't smoke or drink either. Out of the scores of women they know who have gone into the line, the sisters can't think of anyone who has had similar luck. Their aunt eventually found a good man too—a Sikh doctor—but he was married and had a family. He didn't marry the aunt but maintained her and her children as a second family, in secret from his wife.

Shalini is suspicious of men—what if the man she marries runs off with her money? The sisters start to talk about their parents, who got married as children—he was fifteen and she was twelve. They then tell me the story of a district-level government official who recently got his daughter married at the age of eleven, even though, according to the law, a girl must be eighteen to marry. Someone tipped off the police but by the time they made it to the man's house, he had taken his daughter to the groom's village and quickly got the pheras done.

Every choice about their future open to these three dignified and articulate women is a choice, I realize, determined by men. We say our goodbyes. Back on the road, the headlights pick out a small, dolled-up girl, no older than fifteen, sitting regally on a charpoy in the dark, waiting. A little further off, two boys and two girls are in a huddle, probably discussing rates. A pujari stands silhouetted in the doorway of a small Shiva temple by the roadside. 'The temple is an alibi,' says Mina. The man is both the girls' keeper and their pimp. He ensures that the clients don't mistreat them and he also makes certain that the girls don't run away.

The next day I am back in Mina's village. There is someone she wants me to meet, an old lady whom she calls 'Tai'. Tai makes excellent kajal from pure ghee and burnt matchsticks. Mina wants some of it.

A group of curious children follows us into Tai's old house—a tiny courtyard with a verandah running on two sides. She is lying under a filthy quilt on a charpoy—a small, motionless heap.

'Tai!' screams Mina, because Tai is deaf, and Tai gets up hurriedly. She has a hollowed-out face and there is a large wound scabbing on her forehead, but it's something in her right foot that's troubling her. The foot is swaddled in dirty bandages. She throws aside her quilt, revealing wasted brown shanks. On the wall is a shelf holding an ancient, dust-blackened bottle of medicine and under her bed a thali with a bit of dal left in it. Someone usually brings her lunch.

Despite everything, Tai is still beautiful. She has large, inquisitive eyes, which dominate her small face. She speaks in a normal tone of voice in response to what is shouted at her, thus making her interlocutor appear handicapped rather than herself.

Mina tells me what she knows of Tai's story. Mina had a friend in the village, Pooja, who was married off and went to live with her husband in Delhi. Tai is Pooja's father-in-law's mistress, who outlived

Pooja's mother-in-law and was always treated as part of the family. When everyone died or left and there was no one to take care of her in the family home in Agra, Pooja moved Tai to the village, into her own now deserted home, and got the neighbours to keep an eye on her. Mina looks in on her from time to time. Tai has been running a fever; Mina and Mahendar took her to the hospital yesterday. She is not sure what is causing the problem in the foot, but she thinks it might be connected to the fever.

'It's all the same to Tai whether she's dead or alive,' says Mina affectionately. 'She's returned from death so many times.'

'What's her name?' I ask

'What is your name?' bellows Mina.

'What?' asks Tai, looking confused.

'What is your name?'

'Roopvati.'

Tai belongs to Gorakhpur, a city she describes by saying that its men tend to be simple and straightforward—seedhe. Mina tells me she's heard that Tai has been in the line too but Tai tells us a different story. When she was a young girl, her 'husband'-to-be—a married man—and his father came to Gorakhpur looking for a bride for the youngest boy in the family. When her 'husband' saw Roopvati, he said to his father—give this one to me, we'll find another one for my brother. Roopvati's relatives had warned her that he would throw her into a well.

'But he didn't throw me into a well,' she says tenderly. 'I was fine, I ate everything I wanted to during his reign.'

When her man fell sick, she spent a lakh of rupees on his hospital treatment.

'I just wanted him to get well. I fell at the doctor's feet. The doctor promised me that he would cure him.'

When he died, she had a stone chabutra built in his memory.

Tai explains that she doesn't have any children. When she was five months pregnant, someone did black magic on her by putting blood on her comb. She had a miscarriage and has never had children since.

'How old are you?' I ask Tai.

She looks around at the children gathered near her bed, points to a boy of about fifteen who has brought her some water in a brass pitcher, and says, 'When I was his age, Mahatma Gandhi died.'

Tai remembers going to a large maidan in Gorakhpur with her brother and listening to Gandhi speak. She starts to sing, in a surprisingly strong, clear voice, the sabak or lesson she learnt from the Mahatma: 'Uth jaag musafir, bhor bhayee/ Ab rain kahan jo sowat hai/ Jo sowat hai woh khowat hai/Jo jaagat hai woh paawat hai.' (Wake up wanderer, it's morning/ It isn't night any longer that you sleep/ The one who sleeps loses/ The one who wakes up gains.)

Mina sits down with Tai on her charpoy and Tai gives her some kajal in a small, shiny aluminum dibbi. Then we leave, our large entourage moving off with us, and Tai remains sitting there, staring at us with her astonishing eyes.

Will it end like this for Mina too—alone in some corner, nursing only sickness and memories? Walking back to her house in silence, I suddenly ask her, 'Are you happy, Mina?'

'Of course,' says Mina quickly before anything like emotion can slip through. 'Anyone who leaves the line can only be happy.'

[*Names and some details have been changed.*]

Photo credit: Bulbul Hasan

Anjum Hasan is the author of the novels *Neti, Neti* (shortlisted for *The Hindu* Best Fiction Award; longlisted for the DSC Prize for South Asian Literature and the Man Asian Literary Prize) and *Lunatic in My Head* (shortlisted for the Vodafone-Crossword Fiction Award). She has also written the collection of poems, *Street on the Hill*. Anjum's fiction, non-fiction, and poetry has been widely published in anthologies and journals in India and abroad. She is currently the Books Editor for *The Caravan*.

Durga

(Student of BA and Nursing)

After the sudden death of my father, life became quite difficult. My mother didn't have the means to support my education after fifth grade. Our financial situation was quite dire and continues to be so. But Kishori Prerna Manch has helped us.

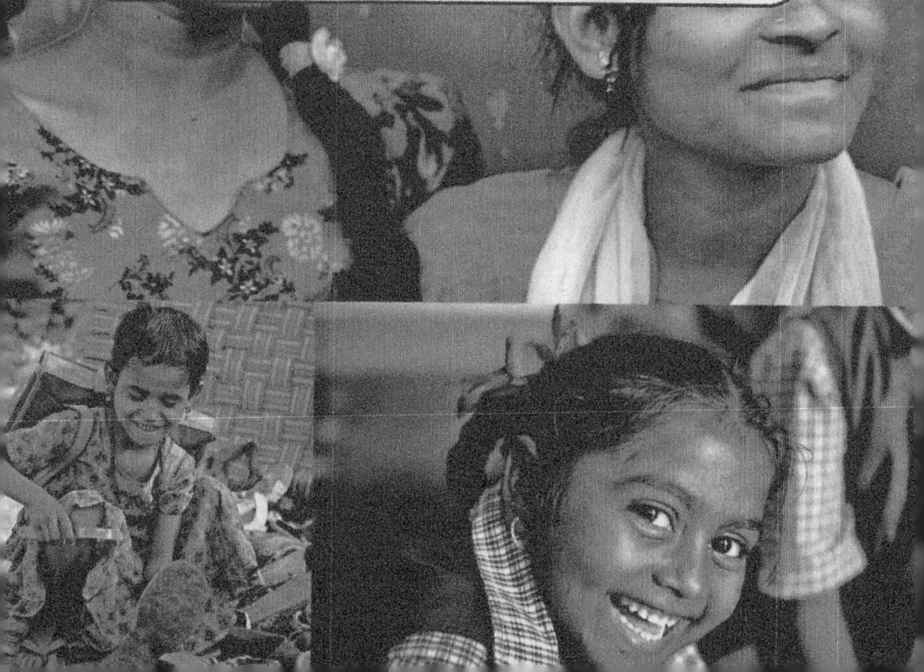

Walk of Life

Shahana Goswami

I've always liked the idea of being in a sea of unknown people, feeding off the energy that you get when you're part of a throng, the buzz, the feeling of belonging, yet being alone and anonymous. The crowd, busy being busy, doesn't intrude into your space but gives you the comfort of knowing they're around. Maybe that's what I love most about Mumbai. Trains, roads, even the seaside for that matter is crawling with people, but no one seems to mind or bother a lonely stranger amid them. I love the freedom to be, to observe, to briefly engage myself with other people's stories and activities, a moment shared without intending to.

It was early June and I was travelling by the local train from Church Gate to Bandra. It was 3 pm on a scorching hot Sunday, perhaps the reason why the train wasn't as crowded as it usually always is. I managed to get a window seat pretty easily. Just as the train was about to leave, a young girl jumped in and came and sat herself right in front of me, as if she had decided her seat of choice beforehand. She looked pleased with herself for having made it on to this train and looked around sheepishly to see if someone had caught her smiling to herself. Her gaze finally rested on me. On realizing that I had not only 'caught' her being pleased with herself but also noticed her looking around to make sure no one had seen her, she broke into a big smile of acknowledgement. I smiled back. She then sat looking out of the window with a lingering smile, and I went back to reading my book. I looked up again and couldn't help but observe this girl. She was a pretty girl and exuded a certain confidence that was mixed with an almost conflicting shyness. She looked as though she was lost in some interesting chain of thoughts. Almost unmindfully I began a conversation, just to tap into her mind, and asked, 'Which class are you in?'

She turned to me and said 'Me?' in a tone of great surprise and then burst out laughing. 'Itni bhi choti nahin hoon main (I am not that young).'

Feeling foolish for having made assumptions about her age, I covered it up with a change of tone and asked her seriously, 'Oh...so what do you do then?'

'Just finished a course in beauty. I'm doing a short mehendi course right now and then will look for a job,' came her dimpled reply.

It was one of those days where I had the time, the mental space, and the inquisitiveness to take this conversation further. We often share our space with people but know absolutely nothing about their lives. I am an urban woman brought up by liberal parents in an environment where I never felt constricted or bogged down by any external pressures, but that is not how most women in our country live their lives. Here I was sitting opposite a girl who I could possibly get to know a little better and understand how an average Indian woman leads her life. It's only in moments like these when you appreciate the advantages you've had in your life, that have allowed you to be who you are. So I jumped at the opportunity, shutting my book completely to make my involvement in this conversation obvious to her, and said, 'A beauty course? What got you interested in a beauty course?'

She shifted in her seat, as if making herself more comfortable for the long conversation that was to ensue, and said, 'Actually na, my eyebrows used to be really bushy and I didn't like the way they made me look. My sisters and my mother suggested I get them threaded because they believed I had a very pretty face otherwise and so they took me to the parlour. After seeing my own transformation, I got interested in the idea of working at a parlour.'

Her frankness was genuine and addictive. I wanted to know everything I could about this girl who so far hadn't failed to surprise me at any instance. My head was swirling with so many questions that I thought I wouldn't even have the space to process her answers. I smiled, shut my eyes for a second to file all my questions in order, and shot them at her one by one, like an interviewer. 'Wait wait wait...let's start at the beginning. When did you decide to work at a parlour?'

'I was eighteen. But I knew that I would need to do some kind of a course. Till I found one, I helped all the ladies in the neighbourhood dress up. Did their make-up for occasions, tied saris for them. Everyone knew who to come to when they needed any beauty related help.'

'When did you finally do the course?'

'Oh, that I did recently, at twenty-three. But now I want to do a mehendi course to make myself better equipped for the job.'

'Twenty-three?' I gasped. 'How old are you now then?'

She giggled and replied, 'Twenty-five.'

'My God! You don't look it,' I said, shocked to find her to be my age and embarrassed to have so confidently assumed she was younger. Given the Indian context, I immediately wondered about her marital status. Most of India, especially a person from her kind of background, would be married with two kids by now. My eyes darted to the parting of her hair and her neck to check for the signs of marriage—the vermillion on her forehead and the mangalsutra on her neck. Noticing their absence I asked, 'And your parents have never put pressure on you to get married?'

'My father died when I was seven and my mother brought up all of us alone in Mumbai, away from the village. We grew up with a different exposure to life than our counterparts in the village. My mother looks at rishtas all the time but she has never pressurized me to marry.'

'So do you not want to marry? Or you just don't like the boys that have come your way?'

'I have nothing against marriage, it's just the difference in upbringing. They are all village boys and I don't find us thinking in the same way. I'm not used to that lifestyle or working in the fields. I doubt I could go and live there now and I think my mother understands that.'

There is so much stigma attached to an unmarried daughter at home because of family and societal pressures, that I was surprised her mother hadn't married her off to the best suitor she could find. Her mother obviously had a lot of faith in her daughter and wanted her to have the life she chose for herself, unlike perhaps how it must have been

Economic Empowerment

In India, GDP could rise by 8 percent if the female/male ratio of workers went up by 10 percent. Within the next two decades or so, the near majority of India's population will be urban.

with her. This girl intrigued me. We were now sitting closer to each other, the train having filled up with four to a seat.

The questions came pouring out of me. I smiled with embarrassment while she answered them for me in a neat narrative that filled all that was lacking in the flow of my questions.

She was the youngest of five children. Her oldest brother had died around the time when the riots broke out in Mumbai. He was very disturbed and soon spiralled into depression. He wanted them to leave Mumbai but they couldn't and his condition kept deteriorating. He became sick and contracted TB and died soon after. She felt sorry about the situation but her tone suggested that she had come to terms with it by now. She told me how her mother chose for them to stay back in the city after her father died because she didn't quite get along with his family. He was an alcoholic and died a pathetic death in the village. They didn't go for his funeral. The strength she drew was always from her hardworking and stable mother, her rock, who worked long hours as a domestic help to bring in the bread so that she could sustain the family and educate her children. I understood why she was so concerned about being economically independent.

Changing the topic from her rather unfortunate family history, I asked about how school was for her.

'I was in school till class—'

'Which stop are you getting off at?' a woman asked her in Marathi. It's a very common practice in Mumbai local trains. They ask you which stop you're riding till, so they can 'book' your seat for themselves and make sure they have a place to sit once you get off. It's like an unsaid norm.

'Bandra,' she said.

The lady asked me the same question and having got the answer from me, she turned to another passenger on her other side (very apparently a stranger to her) and asked her to take my seat from Bandra. She gave me a final look and a questioning nod to confirm that I knew the person I was supposed to offer my seat to. Mumbai never ceases to surprise me with its great sense of bonhomie even on a hot day in a crowded train. But I was too taken in by this conversation to linger for too long on that thought and so I looked straight back at the girl and gave her the look to continue.

'I was in school till Class 7, but after that I had to drop out.'

I assumed it was because she couldn't cope with the curriculum or was not interested in or excited by what was taught at school—something again I was familiar with happening to people coming from families with no history of education.

'No, not at all! In fact I really enjoyed going to school. I was a good student. But the circumstances were such that I was needed at home. My sister had come to home during her pregnancy and there was too much work for my mother to manage alone with no helping hand. I dropped out of school solely for that reason. Even my teachers were very unhappy to hear that I had to leave, and tried their best to convince me to stay. I wish I could have studied more though...'

'So from the age of eleven to twenty-three you were at home doing housework?' She nodded with a smile.

Not wanting to feel sorry for her, I decided to talk about something lighter. 'So what kind of movies do you like? I'm sure you watch a film every holiday you get!'

'That isn't exactly how I spend my holidays,' she said with a giggle. 'I spend time at home, play with my nephews, sometimes go and meet my sisters.'

'You don't like watching films?' I was very surprised because in Mumbai, or anywhere else in India for that matter, there doesn't seem to be a soul who doesn't like going to the movies.

'Well, at home we weren't allowed to watch any on the TV, so I never had a fascination for it. I watch them occasionally with my sisters or my cousins.'

'But you must have a favourite actor, right?'

After a lot of thought (given her obvious lack of interest in films) she said, 'Umm...Akshay Kumar for his fighting and Hrithik Roshan for his dancing.'

We got up as our stop was up next. We made our way through the crowd and stood by the door, while our respective 'seat takers' made their way to our seats. Squeezed between other passengers waiting to get off, I asked her, 'And actress?'

She gave it a few seconds and very decisively said, 'There are no good actresses these days!' We both burst out laughing at the same time.

The train screeched to a halt on the platform teeming with expectant passengers. We were both aware that this conversation would probably end soon, since we were heading in different directions. But I didn't want it to end. She had cast a spell over me with her easy charm and carefree nature.

I was hungry to know more about her. I wanted to further challenge my stereotypical notions about the world through this wonderfully enlightening girl. And without thinking twice I asked her, 'Can I come with you to your house?'

She looked a bit taken aback by that question, and meekly replied, 'Haan, zaroor (Yes, sure).'

'It's just that we've had such a lovely conversation that I wanted it to continue a little longer...maybe see where you live, have a cup of chai...but only if it's okay with you?'

'Haan haan, please,' she said, not looking me in the eye, almost embarrassed that I would think she would refuse. In fact she was very happy and her dimpled smile made it obvious enough.

We were walking towards the east side of the station near the Bandra Terminus when she suddenly turned around and said, 'Bus chalega na aapko? (Will a bus do for you?'. This time I smiled at her stereotyping of the 'well-to-do'. I have travelled in buses since I was five years old. During my college days in Mumbai, I took a bus every day from Andheri to Peddar Road and back.

'Of course,' I said with an understanding smile.

I picked up the conversation thread while we waited for the bus.

'What is your favourite food?'

'Noodles!' She answered with her infectious child-like enthusiasm. 'Earlier it was Maggie but now I like Chinese noodles.' This is what fascinated me about her. Here was a girl who had gone through all kinds of experiences in life, was ambitious enough to do what she wanted with herself, and yet had an almost enviable naivety that made her seem so pure.

The first bus we needed to take had arrived. As we were getting onto the bus she said, 'Whenever I get really angry with my family and sulk, they always cheer me up by getting me noodles.'

We walked to the front of the bus since we had to get off after one stop. I continued, 'And you get angry easily?'

'Yes!' She said, knowing she would surprise me yet again. 'But it's fun when I see them give in to me and win me over with the noodles!' She laughed mischievously, amused and aware of her own antics.

The bus pulled up at the next stop and we got off. 'We have to walk another ten minutes and take the next bus from the other stop.'

I noticed her hands which were covered with delicate orange curlicues. 'Did you do that yourself? It's lovely.'

'Yes,' she said and put them out for me to have a better look. It was beautifully done and she obviously was aware of her talent, which is why she showed off her craft to me with such eagerness. 'I've always put mehendi on my hands and for my neighbours but I want to do it professionally because bridal make-up includes doing mehendi.'

'By the way, how did you find out about the beauty course?'

'I was always on the lookout for it but I knew it would be too expensive to ask my mother to pay for. A friend of mine told me about a course that I could do. I was a bit reluctant because it cost ₹500, which was a bit steep, but my mother was very supportive and helped me out with the fees. She's always wanted me to pursue my dreams. And as luck would have it, there was some sort of a lucky draw and I managed to do my entire course for just ₹100.'

I was deeply pleased to hear that there is justice in the system of luck too. But then again, as many say, luck favours those who fight tooth and nail to make it work in their favour. She had really compelled luck to side with her by keeping her dream alive through all the possible barriers that may have obstructed her path.

'So your mother must feel happy seeing you do so well for yourself. After all, you are finally on your way to being financially independent.'

'Yes, of course, she's happy. She's been there for me in every way. She's such an inspiration for us—working alone, bringing us all up. I just want to make her happy and give her whatever comforts I can. Unfortunately the men in her life have not been able to give her any of it—neither my father, nor my brothers. My sisters used to do whatever they could to ease the financial burdens of the house off her. They have sold koyla (coal), sold water, just to help run the household. But once they got married she's had to look after everything, including my ailing brother's medication. So, yes, I would like to earn enough money, not to be independent, but to be there financially for my mother and contribute to the household.'

I realized how different our approach to money was. We consider taking care of ourselves financially to be a way to take the pressure off our parents. For us it's about being able to fend for ourselves first, and then helping our parents and family. But for her, the self is not separate from the family. Earning a living is only to help out in the household.

'I work at the station in a booth that helps with getting information and drops for polio.' She continued, 'I do it six days in a month and earn enough to take care of all my monetary needs. I want my mother to have an easier life once I start working.'

Suddenly she noticed a 301 go past us, and stop at the bus stop about 100 metres from where we were. Instinctively she started running, screaming out to me, 'Arrey, come quickly, this one doesn't come that often.'

When we had boarded and found ourselves a seat, she asked me, 'Can I ask you a question?'

'Sure,' I said exaggeratedly, trying to make her feel comfortable about asking me anything she wanted to.

'Why are you asking me so many questions? Am I a case study for something? I mean, not that I mind, I'm just curious...'

I felt very sheepish about letting her feel like that. I suppose she was a case study of sorts, a study of a kind of girl I'd never got to know before, a study of life and the way it is for others. I should have realized that my one-sided questioning would perhaps make her feel like an object being examined. It wasn't common for me to get off a train talking to a stranger and make my way to her house. I decided the best thing to do was to tell her exactly what I felt as honestly as I could. At least that would make her feel my involvement in this journey with her, rather than making her wonder about my motives. 'No, you aren't any kind of case study.' I laughed. 'I've never done this before. But something about you made me want to know you better. I don't think I've ever had the opportunity to really get to know a stranger and trust them so completely. And even if I have, I've never exercised it. It wasn't a conscious decision; I'm just going with the flow, just like you've been. Am I right?' I looked at her with a reassuring smile and she smiled back to convey to me that this was exactly what she had hoped to hear.

From the bus window I noticed a shop with leftovers from some previous festivity and asked, 'What is your favourite festival?' just to quickly fill the awkward silence that had set in.

'I like Navratri,' she said very matter-of-factly.

Yes, of course. It is the one festival that involves nine nights of dancing as celebration. Dandiya is a dance with sticks performed in a big group of men and women. It's very playful and vibrant, and is usually a coming together of many strangers.

'For the pujas. I really like praying and any kind of ceremonies that involve prayers to God. Navaratri is the time when there is a lot of puja-paath (rituals and prayers) all day and all night for nine days.'

As soon as I asked her, I knew she was not the kind to enjoy participating in something like Dandiya, since by now I was quite familiar with the pattern of my assumptions about her being totally wrong. Having said that, I still I didn't quite expect this answer. Such a young girl to be so taken in by religion was also not something I considered all that common unless it was in a pursuit to find a good suitor and get married off soon.

'So you enjoy puja-paath that much?' I asked, unable to mask my surprise.

'I find it very soothing. It's calming and makes you feel peaceful, that's why.'

She was not one to follow something blindly and neither would she pray to God to get something out of it, as most young people do. Her idea of being religious was more spiritual and something she had discovered for herself. It wasn't taught to her, it was just what she felt in the presence of God.

In this moment, my mind suddenly wandered for a second to step back from the situation I was in and observe how in about forty minutes of chatting with someone, I felt I knew them enough to assess what they were likely to do or not do. It's funny how you can know people for eons and still not know half the things you end up knowing about a person you spend half an hour talking to incessantly. I'm not sure I knew the answers to many things about my friends, or their take on religion. But with her I knew, not because she told me, but because I realized I now had an instinct for knowing the way her mind works. It's just something I felt in my heart and it made me smile.

'Aap maante ho?' (Do you believe?) Noting my slightly distracted gaze, she clarified. 'Bhagwaan mein...' (In God...)

Just as I was about to answer, she pointed towards the door, indicating we were to get off at the next stop. I thought about my thoughts on God, and though I knew them firmly in my head, I hadn't really had to ever put them in words for anyone else to understand. Without knowing if I had put it all together, I began talking as soon as we got off the bus.

I do believe in God but I'm not sure in what form. I believe there is a force that monitors the ways of the world based on the actions and reactions that naturally exist. It's more like the force of the universe, which keeps everything in balance. Another side of God to me is the voice in my head. I feel like I can talk to him, get advice from him, chat with him whenever I want, and there seems to be a distinct voice that doesn't quite sound like me yet must be a part of me, to be coming from within me.

I trust God as the force of nature that will always try and do what is best for the universe. And since I am a part of the universe, he will also look out for my best interest, by guiding me to make the right choices through my instinct.

Suddenly realizing I had got a bit carried away with my monologue and not bothered to check if the poor girl I was talking to even understood what I was saying, I asked her apprehensively, 'Did I make any sense?'

'It's very unlike any explanation I've ever heard about anyone's belief in God, but I like it. It seems a lot more believable than what people preach religiosity to be.'

We were now walking down the lanes of her neighbourhood, and I noticed that it consisted predominantly of Muslim families. Communal divide, though faint in Mumbai, is definitely something deep-rooted at a subconscious level in all Indians. We are too varied a culture and constantly feel the need to associate ourselves with one community, by alienating ourselves from the others. 'We are the only Hindu family in this neighbourhood,' she said, as though she had read my mind.

I wondered if it bothered her and was pleased to know it actually didn't at all. They have been there for her family in their times of need, sometimes even before any relative could. She told me how they all look out for each other. They live as a community of people, not segregated by religion. All festivity is celebrated alike and together. It's just that people back in her village don't understand this interdependency. They point fingers at her mother for being a single mother, living away from her in-laws and raising three girls in the big bad city of Mumbai, that too in a predominantly Islamic neighbourhood. But she herself is very clear—the world isn't divided into people from different communities; it's just divided into good people and bad people.

We reached her house—a neat little flat on the ground floor with a clothesline adorning the entrance.

'Mummy must still be at work. Can I make you chai?'

'Please. That would be lovely,' I said, quite aware of her excitement at my visiting her house.

The flat opened out into a small living room area. Pictures of gods and goddesses hung on the green-blue walls. The room was sparsely furnished with a diwan, a couple of stools, and a small side table, making the room feel as spacious as possible. She asked me to sit in the living room while she made the tea, but I insisted I would give her company in the kitchen and followed her in. Then I realized why she wanted me to be seated; the kitchen was too small to fit two people in comfortably. I decided to stand by the door of the kitchen and still be near her rather than sit alone in the living room.

Just then a young boy walked down the stairs on one side of the living room and, pushing me aside, went straight towards her. This was her elder brother's son who had been staying with them since both his parents died. Strangely, he bore a significant resemblance to his aunt. She asked him if he wanted his favourite biscuit to which he firmly nodded, took the biscuits, and disappeared outside.

She handed me a nice, strong, milky cup of tea and walked me to the living room. She darted back into the kitchen and reappeared with a plate of biscuits and some namak paras.

'Are your friends all from your neighbourhood?' I asked, realizing I knew nothing about her social life. I had only enquired of her family and of her work.

'I don't really have any close friends. I mean...I have friends from the polio booth and some in the neighbourhood too, but not to go out and spend time with.'

'Don't you miss that?'

'No, I don't, actually. I am close to my mother and my sisters. I find the kind of activities people my age indulge in to be a waste of time. They like roaming around aimlessly, going around with boys...that doesn't interest me at all.'

'So what does interest you?' I said, excited and fascinated by her uniqueness.

'I love kids. I like being around kids and around old people. They have so many interesting stories to tell, and you can learn so much from them. Also, they're lonely and it's nice to be to be able to give them some company.'

'No boyfriends?' I asked, teasing her.

'No,' she said shyly, but went on to explain in a confident tone, 'we don't have the culture to choose our own partners. My mother will let me choose from the proposals that come to us but she wouldn't be okay if I were to tell her I had found someone for myself. People talk, you see. My sisters and I have been very careful to not let my mother's reputation be marred in any way. It's been tough on her as it is, being a single mother. The last thing we need is for our rash decisions to be blamed on her not being able to control her daughters.'

'That's completely understandable.' I took a minute to take in her very mature outlook to life, but was curious to know more about her notions of a life partner and so I asked her what kind of husband she'd want.

She replied without any coyness, 'Someone who doesn't drink and do wrong things. A person who is good to me and my mother.'

I smiled to myself, pleased to get the kind of intelligent and practical answer she gave me, but I wasn't done testing her just yet. 'So what if you got this ideal husband and he earns enough for you both, would you still want to work?'

'Yes, of course! Why would I waste the education I've got? It's for me to feel like I've done something with my life. In fact I wanted to finish my tenth standard exams through correspondence so I can be better equipped to apply for different jobs.'

I wished I had half her ambition in life. I was proud of her and had no doubt that her mother must be as proud, if not more.

'Your mother must be really proud of you, no?'

'Yes, she is. My sister too. They didn't have it this easy and I know their struggles have paved the path for me. They have all been so supportive in letting me realize my dream. They don't want me to miss out on life like they did. And that's all I really want—to be known for doing my job well, to be respected and trusted. If I could achieve this, I will have realized my dreams.'

I looked at her with the belief that she would see that day very soon.

We had finished our chai and the conversation had reached a comfortable end. I thought how strange it was that this stranger had found her way into my heart. She gestured towards the cup in my hand and as I gave it to her I said, 'I should make a move now...'

She smiled and told me that it was one of the loveliest days she had had in a very long time. I hugged her and just as I was walking away, I noticed the road was flecked with the soft pitter-patter of rain. I looked back at her to see if it was just me or if it really was the first shower of the monsoons. She looked up at the sky and smiled and gave me my answer.

'Do you like the rains?' I hollered out to her.

'I love it!' she shouted back.

As if right on cue it began to pour! I took a few more steps ahead but I remembered something, so I quickly turned back, hoping she was still there. Seeing she was, I shouted out, 'Arrey, I forgot to ask you...'

'Sunita,' she said, and laughed out loud.

I realized then that she had probably waited all afternoon for me to ask her this one simple question.

Shahana Goswami was born and brought up in Delhi. She is an actor who has worked in films such as *Rock On* and *Firaaq*. She has recently finished working on Deepa Mehta's adaptation of Salman Rushdie's *Midnight's Children* and will also be working with Khyentse Norbu on a film based on a short story written by Sunil Gangopadhyay. Though not a voracious reader (yet), she is addicted to certain writers, such as Haruki Murakami, who is her favourite.

Jyoti

(Fashion assistant at Pantaloons)

Jyoti is a very simple and soft-spoken girl belonging to a not-so-well-to-do family consisting of her mother, father, younger brother, and two sisters. One of her sisters is married but lives with them as she has filed a divorce case. Jyoti has completed her schooling and now wants to pursue graduation. She wants to work for some time and save money so that she can fulfil the wishes of her sisters, who dreams of getting a respectable job in the near future, as well as for her own studies and independence. Jyoti feels that she is now mature enough to handle certain responsibilities of her own and her family.

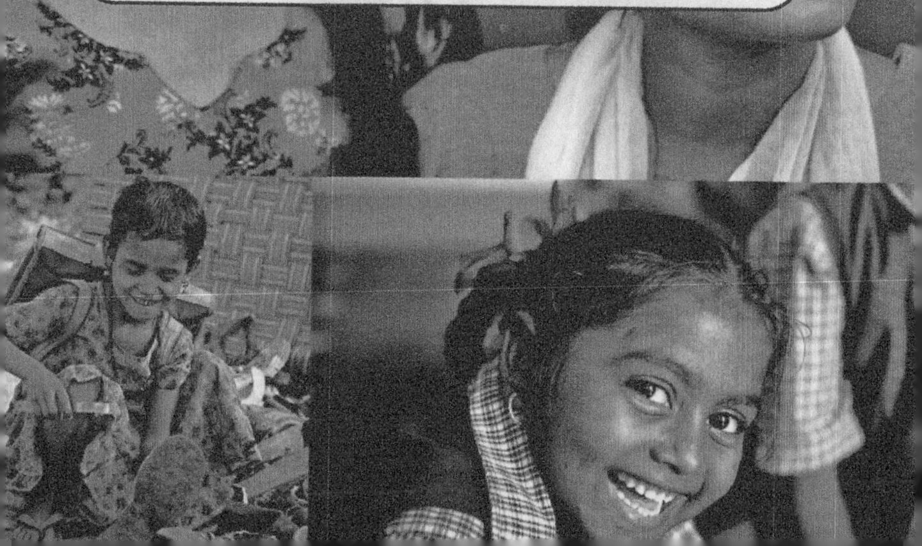

Any Other Sort of Teenager

Meenakshi Reddy Madhavan

This is not a life-changing story. This is not the kind of story where I tell you that I was able to do something to make someone's life better, where you'll gasp at the twist in the tale. It's just the story of one meeting in a lunch home with a tall, shy girl, who told me of her love for tomato curry and chapattis, who answered all my questions with a shrug, a soft 'yes' when I asked her if she enjoyed her job, an even softer 'no' when I asked if she wanted to be married at all. Truth be told, this story, Radha's story, didn't leave me very much to work with. She spoke to me politely for half an hour, leaving me with only two pages of notes but, more importantly, a world to think about.

Radha's parents had lived in Hyderabad for as long as she could remember. When she was young, she had been left in the guardianship of her mother's older sister and her husband, with the understanding that they would send her to a school in the village, and when the time was right, she'd move to the city to join her parents and help them out. When Radha turned fourteen she finally came to the city, but instead of the parents she'd dreamt of, she found an old couple, strangers, who went to work every morning, and left Ashok, her little brother, in Radha's care. Her father was grouchy but a kind man who liked children, and her mother was a sharp-tongued woman who went on about only one thing—Radha's marriage.

'He is a good man,' said Radha's mother. 'He will make you a good husband.'

Radha made a face. Not the kind of face her mother would notice, though sometimes it felt like her mother had eyes at the back of her head.

As if on cue her mother said, 'There's no need to make that face. I am your mother and I know what's best for you.'

Radha finished her morning chores, setting the clothes out to dry at the back of their one-room house, handing her little brother a glass of milk before he went to school, and stopping to check herself in the tiny mirror in the front room. 'I have to go to work now,' she told her mother.

'You won't have to work if you marry him,' her mother retorted.

'I don't want to marry him,' said Radha. The thought made her feel sick.

'He will make you a good husband,' she said.

'And what better man to marry than someone from your own family, you silly girl?'

Her mother wanted her to marry her brother—no, not Radha's brother but Ram Mama. Her uncle. Her almost brother. Because he had been a teenager when she was born, and he had saved her from the snake, and he loved her like a younger sister. And he was her *friend,* at least he had been, till she grew up and everything had to change.

Radha ignored this, adjusted her dupatta, and set out for the bus stop. Walking through Shahpur Nagar, the 'rehabilitation area' allocated to people like them, she thought once more of the village where she was born. 'Once more' would be wrong. She thought of the village often—the hot, dusty road that led into it, the thorn trees lining the walkways, which offered several places to hide, as she did with her friends, making makeshift playhouses, where they sat with their dolls and played at 'House' or 'When I go to my husband's'. Radha had not been such a big fan of the latter game, but her friends enjoyed it. And more often than not, she was cast into the role of the mother-in-law—mean, demanding, who was defeated eventually by the loving capableness and gentleness of her son's wife. Not to mention beauty. All the girls were convinced that as soon as they turn sixteen, they'd be beautiful like the heroines of the films—brown skin would turn magically light, bare, square feet would become little and delicate, incapable of walking the long, arduous village roads without shoes. Their husbands would be like the Telugu superstar, Chiranjeevi, moustached and insouciant; he would pinch at the fat between their sari blouse and petticoat and sing suggestive songs while they fetched the water from the well.

Radha walked past the whitewashed buildings. 'Why is everything in the city so dirty?' she remembered asking her parents when she first came here. 'Where are the houses of blue, green, and yellow?' In her house in the village, there had been a central courtyard with rooms around it; one room was just hers, all hers, and one had been her uncle's. She shook her head. Now was not the time to think of her uncle, Ram Mama, who had been fifteen when she was born, and who often told her stories about how he saved her from a snake when she was two. He had chanced upon her in his room, where she had been explicitly told not to go, squatting in the corner by the cupboard and desk while the cobra swayed menacingly in front of her. 'I didn't have time to think,' he told her, but he had moved faster than he ever had and snatched her up just as the cobra struck at the spot she had been. 'I saved your life, young Radha,' he used to say, laughing, pulling at her braid. 'When you get married to a rich man, tell him that if it wasn't for your uncle, you wouldn't be making him happy.'

As she walked through the street, she passed the usual cluster of boys, well, young men really, who stood around there, at all hours of the day, only leaving when it was time to eat, and whose sole purpose it was to yell things at her as she made her way to work. She was younger or the same age as most of them, but unlike her they didn't have jobs, and watching her, dressed in her 'office suit' of a brown salwar kameez with a gold and brown dupatta (blue on alternate days) made them angrier than if she had actually stopped and spat at their feet. They had been raised to believe they were their parents' shining hope, and yet the world didn't seem to think so. There they were, young men who couldn't get a job, and there she was, a *girl*, making more money than any of them. Probably even more money than their parents.

It wasn't just the attitude of these boys Radha had noticed ever since she got her 'proper office job' with a computer and a cell phone; reactions to her across Shahpur Nagar had been mixed. Some asked her to look out for likely jobs for their children, but most people either avoided her or spoke in low voices when she was around, shutting up when she drew close. Once, she had answered her cell phone in the middle of an evening gathering, and the whole crowd had gone silent, watching her with hostile eyes. 'Putting on airs,' someone had mumbled and after that, Radha hid her cell phone, using it only when she was alone. It didn't help that her parents, after getting over the initial shock of their daughter getting a job, used every instance to rub it into people's faces. 'Bring your phone, Radha, and show aunty,' her mother would say, sitting on the steps with a neighbour, drinking tea, and Radha would watch aunty's face grow taut and her throat constrict as she swallowed the words she no doubt wanted to say: 'What's so great about Radha, when it could have been *my* son? *My* daughter?' She wished the young men had the class to swallow their words too, but it was their way of making themselves feel better and above her, because they were *men* and she was a girl. 'Oho, Miss Office, think you're so big!' yelled the gang leader and the rest followed suit, catcalling and hooting, till she was out of sight. She hated it, she hated them, but the only way to avoid them was to quit her job, and she couldn't, or wouldn't, do that. She felt almost like she was defying them all, the stupid boys and the interfering neighbourhood aunties.

It had not always been this way for Radha. She had always been a dreamer, and when she was thirteen or fourteen, she dreamt of someday having a big house, with a couple of chickens, a goat, a few children, who she would dress neatly and send off to school. She had dreams for her parents too, how they would eventually get sick of the city life and come back to the village, her father tilling a small plot of land, her mother walking to the temple with her aunt, and her little brother, eventually, tending to the many buffaloes her father would buy.

It was only as she got older that she realized that these dreams would never come true. Her parents were never going to be landowners. Her maternal grandfather had been somewhat well off, but this money passed on to his son, Ram Mama. Her father, with his job in the chemical plant, would be working there till his last breath. Or till her little brother finished with school and got a job of his own. She was not counted as a wage earner for the family, not really, even though now she was making enough money to add nicely to the family kitty. One half kept aside for her dowry, the other saved for her younger brother's college tuition, so that he could get a well-paying job, and then marry a girl from a comparatively wealthy family who would bring in a sizeable enough dowry that her parents could live off for the rest of their lives. No buffaloes. No walks to the temple.

Radha and her parents are migrant workers. They are people who come from villages to the city to look for jobs, drawn to the bright lights like moths. People who think, 'Well, anywhere has got to be better than here', as they leave their poor villages and unfertile lands. People who speak about how factories have plenty of work for able-bodied people like them, but secretly dream of being the next success story, passed down from generation to generation: 'You know, when your grandfather went to the city, he went with *nothing*, just the shirt on his back and ₹5. And look at him now!'

I realize how special this young girl sitting in front of me is. For every girl like Radha, there are

Migration

Number of migrants (in millions)

1951–61	66
1961–71	68.2
1971–81	81
1981–91	80.9
1991–2001	98.3

thousands more who cannot even get close to a good office job. Yet her parents are insistent that she follow her destiny, and as a woman, her fate is simple—she has to be wed. I can sort of see their point of view; they wouldn't be considered good parents if they didn't settle her down with a respectable man who earned a decent amount of money. It was their job to see their daughter happy, but they were somewhat blind to the other happiness she could have, the happiness springing out of doing a job well and having work that you love.

'Off to work?' asked someone beside her. Radha looked up to see her friend Sachin, and smiled.

She had five friends, and was always surprised by it. Back in the village, she hadn't thought about how many friends she had; it was something she took for granted. How foolish she had been. In her first few weeks in the city, she would sit outside the house and dream about her home in the village. The call of the temple bells, her best friend Susheela, who had just become a woman, and whose ceremony would have been happening right about then. Her own passage to womanhood had been marked by a feast and also by the counsel from her guardian, her mother's older sister, who had taken her aside and told her not to spend that much time alone with her uncle. 'You're a woman now, it doesn't look nice.' As if it would have made a difference to Ram Mama whether or not she was a woman. She felt just the same way as she had before the bleeding started, but he seemed to understand what her aunt was implying, and besides giving her a gold chain he hadn't said much else.

They walked past the building which housed some of the young men in the area, all come to earn their living in the fertilizer factory before sending for their wives. Radha tried to imagine their wives—little, uneducated things, who would soon be resigned to a life of baby bearing and doing odd jobs once they were in the city. Most of these men were daily wage workers, who came to the city looking like their mother's darling sons and after a week of back-breaking labour, looked like the hollow-cheeked, hard-eyed men she had gotten used to. Sachin's parents had been daily wagers too, working themselves to the bone so that he could enjoy the college education they never received. He, in turn, planned on getting a job immediately out of college so that he could take care of them. In the city, you didn't dream the way you dreamt in a village. In the city, things were simple and never wavered; you worked hard, you tried to make your children better workers than you, and then eventually, you died.

Right before they turned off into the main road, she glanced up and saw the graffiti that always pleased her: 'If you have talent, you will become patent, else you will become tenant.' Written, confusingly enough, in English, so not everyone could read it, Radha felt like it was a secret message to her. She wasn't quite sure what it meant, but she had talent, lots of it, and she had no desire to stay on in Shahpur Nagar as a tenant. None of her five friends did. They had dreams too—to have a small house somewhere nice, with their parents finally getting a chance to relax.

Radha got her break when a woman from the Plan office in Hyderabad came around Shahpur Nagar scouting for children for their school. She had explained very nicely that they intended to look after some of the children, offer them drawing classes perhaps, tutor them at school work. It would be better than doing nothing after school. Radha thought she was too old to join their extra classes, and it was a pity, because from the reports, it sounded wonderful. No one was hit for forgetting a lesson, the teachers actually *listened* to you, and you got a *meal*. She'd walk past the makeshift classroom on her way back from school and listen to the happy sounds, the singing, from inside, feeling a little wistful. This might have been her life if she had been born a little later.

One day, the woman from the office came back looking for young girls who were doing well in school. Radha went to the office where she was told, in her own dialect, that she could go to college if she chose. All she had to do was get through a vocational course. They'd pay for it, and help her get a job when she was done. Her time in the city had made Radha sceptical of anything that looked too good to be true. 'We want to work with girls like you,' said the lady in the office. 'We want to help you realize your dreams.' That day, Radha went back home hopefully and told her mother about it. She was fifteen years old, and had just finished school. They couldn't marry her off, not now, not till she was legally an adult, so her mother grudgingly gave her consent. Radha signed up for it immediately.

It was in this college that she met her five friends. Of the six of them, Radha was the first to get a job, so in a hurry was she to start making money, to help, to go back to her village and realize her dreams. It was also here that the lady recognized Radha's potential and sourced a job for her. Her first real job! She beams just at the memory of it and I ask her more about it.

Radha works as a data entry operator for life insurance forms. It isn't much of a job but it is something she can do. She tells me that she likes it. I can't help but imagine her parents who work in the factory, her grandfather who could barely sign his name. She might even be making as much as her Ram Mama. She loves what the job represents—hot lunches for her brother and the luxury of buying whatever she likes at the weekly vegetable market. Once she secretly parted with some of the money to buy a pair of jeans she had seen hanging up at a stall in the same market so that she could look more like the other girls. At home, in a rare moment of solitude, she tried them on, and liked what she saw—a 'modern' girl, a working girl, someone who held her fate in her own hands. She hasn't yet worn them to work, but she wants to. She wants to walk past all the taunting boys in her jeans, wearing them like a shield.

With every minute, Radha surprises me more with her determination and strength. She tells me that no one really has the time or inclination to talk to each other at office so she eats her lunch alone, sometimes at her desk. What she likes is the power of the computer, this *exceptional* machine, its idiosyncrasies which only she knew of, and which her parents wouldn't know how to turn on. I can tell that she is quite proud of herself. This 17-year-old has colleagues who are in their forties. Radha tells me that someday, she might get a nursing degree, and then she'd help the little children she sees on her way to office. Her aunt used to say, 'There's always someone worse off than you.' She dreams of working in a big hospital, with doctors who called her 'Miss', where she'd walk around, calm and composed, administering medicine to the poor and needy. Maybe then her parents would say, 'Why, Radha doesn't need to get married at all, look at all the good deeds she's doing.'

She's now working on her typing skills, trying to be quicker, learning as many short cuts on the keyboard as she can because the faster she works, the more money she earns. She knows that this is not a job she can have forever, and that the older people in the office can barely manage to keep up with the workload. She has started getting headaches already, and her friends tell her that these are computer related, and that she should take a break when she feels them coming on. But who has the time for breaks? Her friends don't understand this because right now their biggest fear is their final exams. Hers is not making her weekly quota. If she doesn't make the money, her brother won't be able to go to college. Her parents will have to work harder to pay the rent. They are a poor family, but a proud one—one that won't resort to begging. At least they have a house and relatives in the village.

When Radha had gone back to the village over the Ugadi holidays, her friends had clustered around her, bombarding her with questions. *Tell us about the city,* they said, *do you see movie stars everywhere? Have you been for a walk around Tank Bund? Have you gone to the Golconda Fort? Eaten at those big-big restaurants?* How was she going to tell them the truth about living in a city? That they, her friends, had a better life than their urban counterparts. That sometimes, depending on which route she took, the bus would go past Tank Bund, and in the evenings, she'd rest her forehead on the sticky bus window and watch couples strolling along and children yelling. She always meant to get off there someday, and go for a walk herself, but somehow, she never found the time.

Once, her friends and she decided to go out for a 'treat'. They chose McDonald's, drawn to the colourful outside and the shiny pictures of the food they could buy. Each of them went over the menu over the cashier's head like it was a textbook, and finally decided on six McVeggie burgers and two small Cokes to share. They hadn't made conversation, being too busy watching the other people, basking in the air conditioner, and taking turns to get the free ketchup from the dispenser. She loved the food but it came second to her favourite tomato curry with chapattis. She tried to describe it to her village friends, but they wrinkled their nose at the thought of it. For them, a feast involved rice and as much curry as you could eat, with vegetables on the side.

And Golconda Fort may as well have been on the moon. About forty minutes out of the city, it would involve taking a whole day off, and she would have to ensure that her parents and brother had the day off too, because she wouldn't dream of going there without them. Then her mother would have to pack a picnic lunch, which would be even more stressful for her, because they'd have to budget in all four of them eating the same meal, not eating the factory provided food, and this would mean more expenses and more division of their money.

Radha had answered their questions with shrugs, smiles, and short answers. 'Yes, I like the city,' she'd say. 'Yes, the buildings are very tall.'

'Sometimes, you can see *foreigners* walking around the streets, like you and me.' She told them about McDonald's, but left out the part where suddenly the six of them were aware of their background, were aware that their clothes were cheap, that they didn't smell quite the same as the others, that they didn't know the right way to eat this food. That, for the first time in her life, she had felt ashamed and small even though she had been an actual college student, well on her way to getting an actual job.

We could not be more different, Radha and I. Except for the accidents of our birth, I too can claim part of my heritage from that part of the country, and I am familiar with the landscapes she speaks about, familiar with the language she speaks. But even though I'm not that much older than her, and like her, work, am a woman, and unmarried, we may as well be different species. I can see this in how she talks to me. Despite my interpreter and my carefully non-invasive questions, her guard is always up; she is somewhat deferring, but the line is drawn between us. At the end of the day, I go home to a house, unmarried, by myself, and make my money to make my life better, not to add to a dowry fund. But ours is not a unique disconnect.

All over India, there's this disparity. Of course, you don't need me to go on about it, you're probably well aware of that yourself. How to wipe out generations of karma? How to wipe out the Indian class consciousness that we are inadvertently taught in our cradles? Radha's mother could be one of many I've encountered on the street, in a local train, on a bus. We might have sat next to each other, bought vegetables at the same vendor, but while Radha's mother and I don't live in the same world, in much the same way my parents and I may not, Radha and I certainly do. So, we'll shoot glances at each other—young woman to young woman—and then, maybe, one or the other of us will look away. It's only because of this meeting with her where I've come to meet my alternate reality face to face, that I think of the other young women who linger in the corners of my vision. Radha has long ago grown into a woman, thinking about her family, making money, and worrying about her future. At her age, I had board exams and my wardrobe to worry about, and, likely, so did you. I'm not blaming us; that is our life, but what strikes me now is what other lives are about, and how priorities can be so very different. And beneath it all, how we take everything we're blessed with for granted.

'How will you stop your parents from marrying you to him?' I ask.

She looks down, and for the first time, her voice isn't soft. She's sure of herself now and smiles as she answers, 'I'll tell him! I'll tell him to say no, and no one will force me to marry him then, because he won't want to.'

'Are you sure he'll listen?'

'Yes, he's my *uncle.*' If she was any other sort of teenager, she would have rolled her eyes at my adult stupidity, but she is polite, quiet, and proud of her plan.

She leaves before us so that she can rush back to work. I want to weave a cocoon of safety and well-being around her, her teenage limbs so gawky and vulnerable, her bright, optimistic eyes, her dupatta wrapped neatly and securely, fastened at her shoulder with pins. I want the world to treat her well. I want her to get her due. I want, in short, for her to have the life she should have, and is being denied, because of a quirk of gender. I never wished I was a boy. Being a girl is *fun*. I want it to be fun for Radha too.

Meenakshi Reddy Madhavan is the author of two books—*You are Here* and *Confessions of a Listmaniac.* She lives in New Delhi and is currently working on her third book.

Sita

(Member, Kishori Prerna Manch, Kharbara, Bikaner)

I feel like a human being after learning how to read and write at the Girls Camp. I was like a dumb animal before that. I'm at a place now where I can achieve my dreams using my education. Otherwise, I would have been married off by now and would be looking after my kids.

I'm determined to be a teacher. But I haven't done my BEd yet. I know I will face a lot of challenges if I decide to pursue BEd.

Born to Die

Pooja Bedi

My favourite morning ritual is to spend an hour reading the papers with a steaming mug of English breakfast tea for company. Scams, scandals, vandalism, political slugfests, tsunamis, and earthquakes; they make me feel really grateful for the life I live. But today was different. Page fifteen carried a story of a healthy newborn girl child who was declared dead a few hours after being taken home from the hospital. One of the many cases of female foeticide. Additional details such as the girl's family taking the baby away without a formal discharge made me wince at the thought of the perceptible hurry they were in to commit the dastardly act. The village, Devra, in Jaisalmer, Rajasthan, is notorious for girl child killings. There are only thirteen girls in Devra, and they are all below the age of ten. What was this news report doing on page fifteen? The frequency of such stories, the gruesome reality, and the degree of such 'socially acceptable' inhumanity makes it far more pertinent, shocking, and needy of attention than the report on page one of another Commonwealth Games fund misappropriation story. I sighed exasperatedly and put down the paper.

As a woman, a mother, and an Indian, I am enraged when I read about atrocities against the girl child. Are we a nation of murderers and savages? The first census in independent India in 1961 showed a sex ratio of 976 while the 2011 Census has thrown up a formidable ratio of 914 girls to 1000 men! In places like Jhajjar in Haryana the ratio is cringeworthy—774 per 1000; it is 830 in Haryana, 846 in Punjab, 859 in Jammu and Kashmir. India is a nation that reveres its 'mothers' and worships goddesses in the form of Lakshmi, Saraswati, Parvati, Durga, and Kali as symbols of wealth, intelligence, strength, and power, and yet we have the highest numbers of female foeticide. Shocking and perplexing!

Here I was, safely ensconced in my penthouse, enjoying a privileged life, one that I have worked very hard for, and surrounded by women friends who have charted equally enviable lives for themselves in various professions, wondering why this country deemed us a liability. Our country has had a woman prime minister and a woman president. We have witnessed Kalpana Chawla going into space, seen women excelling in their chosen fields, be it industry, finance, IT, the corporate world—traditionally, male domains—and yet the numbers of female foeticide are shocking.

With representation in every sphere of work, girls have proved that if you give a girl equal opportunity and education they are just as capable of earning, being self sufficient and resilient breadwinners for the family as their male counterparts. Of course there is the great 'acceptable' divide in India between women and men. Especially when it comes to role playing. The problem in India is that women don't have a distinct individual identity; women here are born as someone's daughter, sister, and become a wife, which eventually leads them to becoming someone's mother. In India, when is a woman someone in her own right? By tradition we push her into subservience and role playing, don't educate her because she'll be too smart for her husband or, alternately, get her a degree for the purpose of bagging her a 'suitable groom', and then put her formidable degree to work in the kitchen and in child-rearing. Women in India are still trapped in the medieval feudal set-up. Yup! The same India that saw women fight side by side for their independence from the British sixty years later sees its women fighting for the right to be born.

Indian women are so attuned and well brought up for role playing that it allows very little room for individuality and for her to reach her full potential. She is allowed to go out and be the co-provider, but it is still expected that she come home and be the nurturer, keep traditional values alive in a modern environment. Some women work because they have to, some because they want to, but in both cases it's tough, because in India women have to delicately balance their home life and traditions with job demands.

Of course I am continually amazed by the modern Indian working woman. She is an incredible phenomenon because no matter how high the expectations are of her, she still does all of it. Given an opportunity, most Indian women not only perform, they outperform. 'So, why the horrific bias?' I asked myself repeatedly as I got off the breakfast table and headed to work.

My thoughts all day kept revolving around a woman watching her girl child being born and killed within a day. How did the mother endure the agony of such a brutal loss? What makes a woman so unwanted? Aren't we all glad that our mothers weren't killed at birth?

As I grabbed my to-do list for the day, slipped into my high heels, and shot out the door, I reminded myself that though the reporting of such practices largely highlighted villages and small towns, female foeticide is also rampant in the big cities, and these were cases which generally went unreported. In fact, when I see the statistics on disproportionate gender imbalances in the metros, and also, shockingly, that cosmopolitan South Mumbai fares no better, I realize it has everything to do with warped attitudes and perspectives, and very little to do with geography.

As my car zipped through the streets of Mumbai, I noticed a beggar combing out the knots in her daughter's hair. I frowned at the thought of the mother–daughter duo begging on the streets. The child should be in school. Did the mother not want a better life for her daughter? It's time we all realized our incredible power as women, to give birth, alter lives, and create and shape societies.

As I got out of the car and walked down the busy road, I looked at the hordes of women walking around me. I like to think that there are millions of women who will possibly take advantage of their strength as women, hold hands with other women, and stand up for other women. A movement of women, by women, for women! I wanted to be a part of it. I wanted to do something that would impact the lives of a million women. It's all very well to advocate from afar, but what I needed to do was let one woman from the progressive lead the million by example. Every time I read about rape, sexual abuse, and molestation, it angers me because men are perpetrators of such crimes, not women. But gender disparity ratios anger me doubly because it shows the hand of a woman's consent in aiding the death of girls. Regressive patterns exist only because each one of us allows it to blossom in our own homes. I wanted to meet a woman who was persona non grata for having a girl child and was someone who had the strength to fight back.

Over the next few days I made many calls and finally got in touch with Plan India. Plan is one of the world's largest community outreach organizations, and one of their specific goals, in India, is to empower children and women. They identified for me a woman in Uttar Pradesh who had been subjected to brutal humiliation by her husband for bearing a third girl child. I was moved by her resolve to not have more children in the quest to produce a son, and the fact that she had stood her ground in the face of abuse and great pressure. I signed up with them and made plans to head to UP.

I arrived in Lucknow feeling quite like an investigative reporter embarking on a sting operation. The only difference being, I told myself, that I was exposing a malaise this family was apparently open to talking about. As my car veered off the main road into the dusty, narrow streets, I was excited at the prospect before me. The car finally came to a halt in front of a small house and I was led into a bare and simple meeting room. The house was teeming with people, and my head spun with the different names and details I was bombarded with as I handed them the boxes of mithai and biscuits I had brought for the family. However, Pushpa, who I had come to meet, wasn't among them.

The family seemed very happy to have me visit their home. They chattered animatedly about my reality shows and films, my children, and Mumbai, but after a while I wondered about the absence of Pushpa and whether, like with the mafia, these were filters to suss me out and to protect and insulate Pushpa from any harsh interrogation. After twenty minutes of chitchat I decided to cut through the circle of defences, and enquired gently about Pushpa's whereabouts. There was silence, and then the family said she was coming, but that she wasn't in a very stable emotional state as it had been only a few weeks since her child had died. They informed me that the child had fallen very ill and could not be saved.

I was filled with disbelief and scepticism. We so often hear of girl children being poisoned, suffocated, drowned, buried alive...and knowing,

Female Infanticide

The data reveals that in the age group 0 to 6 years, the gender ratio is 914 girls to 1000 boys. Which means, for every 1000 boys, there are at least 60–70 girls who are killed before or within six years after birth.

prior to my visit, of Pushpa's husband Kamlesh's aversion to this third girl child, I felt uneasy and unsettled. All of a sudden the room filled with the presence of Ramrati, Pushpa's mother-in-law, a 61-year-old uneducated woman and clearly the ruler of the roost. She was mother to five children—three daughters, Rita, Gita, and Sunita, who were present in the room, and two sons, Mithilesh and Kamlesh, both absent from this gathering. Ramrati's smiling entry temporarily distracted me from the uneasiness I felt on hearing about the death of Pushpa's little girl child. There was something warm and lovely about Ramrati's demeanour and the way her three daughters looked at her with adoration.

Ramrati's daughters told me about their lives. Rita, the first born, had had an arranged marriage and was now mother to two girls and one boy. The other two sisters, Gita and Sunita, both of whom works with an NGO, Vatsalaya, laughed hysterically as they told me about the dreadful marriage proposals that came for Rita, and the problems they had shooing the unwanted suitors away. It was after this that they had decided, as a family, that henceforth it would be easier if they married out of choice. I looked around at the room filled with smiling family members, a bit confused. I had come for tales of atrocities and an exposé on female foeticide but what was being presented was a very unique lower middle class family, which was a living example of the changes we'd like to see in the rigid and often feudal Indian family structure. Ramrati beamed from the sofa she had sunken comfortably into and added that all her children had married of their own choice. I was still a bit mystified. Of course, times have changed dramatically. Nowadays it's commonplace in urban India to have love marriages but uneducated Ramrati of Lucknow, at sixty-one years of age, was clearly way ahead of her time. And it seemed, as the stories continued, that her permissiveness did not end only at love marriages.

The youngest daughter, Sunita, fell in love with a man from a different caste, and while Ramrati supported the relationship, the final say rested with her father, who was also completely supportive of the union. Ramrati's husband, a gentle, simple man and the patriarch of the family, nodded vigorously at the memory. He had been quiet the whole time, and this was his first sign of participation. Breaking away from the tradition of marrying into caste and community was a huge deal for a family such as this. Furthermore, it turned out that the three girls were married when they were approximately twenty-eight or thirty years of age. This was astonishing, especially when girls in urban India are still pressurized to get married after turning twenty-five! What next, I wondered? How many more surprises?

The seemingly endless wait for Pushpa was peppered with more laughter and love stories. Gita shyly revealed that she had met her husband in 1990 and married him twelve years later in 2002. I looked on in disbelief. A twelve-year romance? That was something no traditional family would be able to handle without pressurizing her to get married. Gita grinned and said that the family had no clue about the courtship, and they had never forced her to find a groom during all those years. Gita gave birth to her first child after seven years of marriage and has been very happy with just one girl child. She firmly added that she and her husband had no intentions of having another child for the sake of having a son. No desire for a boy? I probed. No pressure from your family, or perhaps from his?

Sunita piped in to say that the only gender bias she experienced while growing up was that Rita, Gita, and her being girls, were more pampered and got more attention from their parents. Ramrati chuckled and added that when her girls were born her husband distributed five times more alms and sweets than he had done when his sons were born.

Something didn't quite fit. All this talk about loving girls didn't quite fit. It wasn't the story I was tracking. If they were such a liberal family, why then did Ramrati's youngest son trouble and torment his wife for a son? Did the youngest of his daughters really die of an illness? How were his other two daughters treated?

Almost on cue two little girls entered the room. Muktanjali, age thirteen, came carrying a tray laden with steaming cups of tea, while Bhumika, age nine, shyly followed and sat down beside her. I observed Bhumika closely. With her short cropped hair and jeans she could have easily passed off as a boy. Is it a sign of being progressive that their girls can have short hair and wear jeans (which none of the other women of the house did), or is it an attempt to make her 'boy-like', I wondered. I asked them if they were enjoying their studies and what they wanted to be in life. In a trice Muktanjali said 'engineer' with a smile, while little Bhumika piped up with 'I am going to be a doctor'. In middle-class India it is every parents' dream that their *son* will grow up to be an 'engineer' or a 'doctor'. It was a major shift in attitudes that the girls had picked 'masculine' career choices and that the family encouraged the equality of the sexes by allowing such dreams to flourish.

Ramrati didn't need to resort to bra-burning histrionics to give her girls their freedom of choice. Quietly, solidly, and intelligently she has ensured that all the women of the house, her daughters and daughters-in-law, were given the opportunity to realize their full potential. Pushpa and the other sister-in-law may have been given chores such as making the bed, cleaning the house, and helping in the kitchen, but Ramrati also ensured that their education did not stop after they married her sons, and that they were treated on par with her daughters. Despite her lack of education, Ramrati used her position as matriarch to change every woman's reality in that household progressively. But then what gave rise to her son's anti-girl child stance? How did it develop with such progressive and permissive parents? What did Ramrati have to say about it? Before I could enquire into the details, there was a hush as Pushpa finally drifted into the room. I use the word 'drifted' because she came in like a ghost. Sad, dejected, her eyes vacant, she sat gingerly on a chair.

I didn't how to react. She was clearly in a state of grief because of the recent death of her youngest child. How much had she endured for bearing a third girl child? I reached for her hand and locked eyes with her. 'How are you doing, Pushpa?' I gently asked. There was a flicker in her eyes. Sensing her fragility, the sister-in-laws immediately surrounded her and as their arms wrapped around her, Pushpa's eyes welled with tears and she retreated within herself.

I felt awful. Like I had brutally invaded her home, her life, her emotions, and her fragile reality. That I was forcefully opening a Pandora's box of experiences for her that she would probably have liked to keep buried. If this was emotionally testing for me, I don't think I could even begin to comprehend how gruelling this must be for her. Her husband's sisters, mother, the two daughters that she had given birth to, and other family members fidgeted uncomfortably. Being a mother myself, I took a decision to end the conversation at this point. I did not want Muktanjali and Bhumika, both of whom looked crestfallen, to see their mother weep or hear certain damning details, which my questioning might throw up. Besides, I wondered, how easy would it be for Pushpa to openly condemn or expose her husband in front of his family? There was something that they weren't telling me, but I knew that this wasn't a good time to ask. I finished what was left of my tea in a big gulp, hugged Pushpa tightly, and thanked the family members for their hospitality. Before leaving I told Pushpa that I would like to meet her alone the next day.

She seemed as dejected and fragile as she had been the previous day. It also seemed evident that she had been crying just before I walked in. Fortunately this time we had arranged the meeting at the office of a local NGO, so there were no family distractions. We ordered some masala chai and biscuits in the hope of lightening up the atmosphere. A little bit of chitchat about Lucknow city, our hotel, and mouth-watering tunday kababs got Pushpa to take her eyes off the floor and actually engage in a conversation with us. If I had come to Lucknow hoping for a firebrand mascot to champion the cause of the girl child, I was wrong. It occurred to me that if all of Ramrati's children had had love marriages, there must have been some wonderful moments to have given Pushpa reason enough to commit to Kamlesh. Hoping that happy memories might help cheer her up and initiate the process of sharing her journey, I thought it best to take Pushpa back to how she met Kamlesh and work forward from there. So, to dispel the sombre mood I smiled and told her that I wanted to know everything about her first meeting with Kamlesh.

She started softly, but as memories started tumbling out of long forgotten spaces her voice got stronger. She was nineteen years old when she had gone as a tourist to Dorahat, a little ahead of Ranikhet. Kamlesh was her brothers' classmate and it was love at first sight for the two of them, much to the consternation of her family, she added. Ramrati may have been a progressive matriarch who looked beyond forged alliances and caste, but Pushpa's family was aghast. Hers was a patriarchal family comprising four brothers, who were enlisted in the police and military service, and two sisters all of whom had married within their caste. And there was Pushpa, a Thakur caste girl wanting to marry a scheduled caste boy! It was like a scene from a Bollywood film. Their clandestine five-month romance of stolen moments together, writing letters to each other, and phone calls ultimately led to their marriage in an Arya Samaj temple with none of her family members present.

Perhaps she would have been better off if she had just married as per her father's wishes, I thought. I stared at Pushpa who seemed lost in her thoughts and tried to objectively analyse her reality. One, Pushpa's mother had died when Pushpa was just thirteen years old. Would the family attitudes have been shaped any differently if her mother had been alive? Would Pushpa have been able to complete her education and work in the state-run Balvikas organization like she did today? The second thing that occurred to me was that given her conditioning, upbringing, and the fact that her brothers were in positions of power that they could have used against her, it was very courageous of Pushpa to have eloped with the man of her choice. Later, when she was five months pregnant, Pushpa went back to visit her father and brothers who were so delighted with the news that they immediately opened their arms and welcomed their 'errant' daughter back into their fold. If Muktanjali had reunited mother and family while still unborn, her birth was a source of incredible happiness for both families.

Under normal circumstances in a traditional family, baby number two would have come along shortly after, but under Ramrati's insistence, Pushpa, twenty-one years old, took a break from baby making and continued her education. She only gave birth to her second daughter, Bhumika, five years later. Once again the entire family was delighted and celebrated her arrival with much gusto, presents, and band baaja. I asked Pushpa about her husband's reaction. Just as I had expected, Pushpa's smile faded and her eyes lost their joy. I gently reminded Pushpa that she must tell her story, no matter how difficult, because it would help countless other women to deal with similar situations. Pushpa looked at me wryly, fidgeting with the edge of her shawl, and said that Kamlesh had dearly wanted a son. After all, his brother Mithilesh had two children, both of them sons.

I was relieved that Pushpa had finally opened up to talk honestly about her situation. I enquired whether there was any room for Kamlesh's ridiculous demands in a home that respected women and treated them as equals. How, I asked Pushpa, did Ramrati feel about her son's boorish behaviour? Pushpa enlightened me, very matter-of-factly, that no one could persuade her headstrong husband into thinking or doing something he didn't want to. As a child, when Kamlesh didn't want to go to school, nothing in the world could make him. You could break eight rulers on him but he stood steadfast and stubborn. He had also displayed the same obstinacy when it came to marrying Pushpa. Kamlesh's notion of his power and position in the household was based on nothing else except the fact that he was male. There are two types of fighters—

ethical fighters and bullies. Ethical fighters are those who fight for what they think is their right, and to protect those that cannot defend themselves. Bullies just throw their weight around and misuse their physical strength or positions they are given. While, on the one hand, it was commendable that Kamlesh had had stood up for his lady love and taken his commitment respectably to the altar, it could also be that it was a macho showmanship of 'marrying up' in caste. Pushpa deprecatingly divulged how Kamlesh had hysterical outbursts when his sisters attempted to wear jeans and how his obstinacy on the issue, led incredibly, to a physical fight with family members, with him maintaining that they were corrupting the girls. 'Bigaad rahe ho in sab ko,' he had screamed in a fit of rage one day, pushing the family members into submission to maintain the peace. Yet, I reflected, it seemed fine to him that his daughters wore jeans and had cropped hair. Kamlesh seemed, to me, to fit the category of the family bully.

For all the colours that Pushpa had brought into her own life, she had married the black sheep of Ramrati's family. The neutral location, the tasty masala tea, and our concern seemed to have worked because Pushpa was now opening up to me, almost as if the words once out unburdened her and lifted a weight off her weary shoulders. She spoke about Kamlesh's histrionics, drunken brawls, and regressive attitude, which were, more often than not, fuelled by his group of friends. She rued the fact that her husband's show of strength and aggression was in fact induced by an incredible dependency on his friends' views and perspectives. They were, in her eyes, a ridiculous group of men who thought their masculinity lay in hanging out together, playing cards, drinking together, producing male heirs, and revelling in being 'men'. Whenever Kamlesh returned home drunk, egged on by the drunken banter of his friends, and fought with his family, he would use the fact that he had only daughters as an excuse for his state. Whenever his brother Mithilesh would try to intervene and calm him down, Kamlesh would double his display of aggression and inevitably tell his brother to back off because he would never understand his pain. After all, Mithilesh had two sons, so how could he ever understand how difficult it was to be the father of two girls.

And that's when the pressure mounted on her to have another child, Pushpa tearfully revealed.

The memories of all that followed subsequently must have come upon her like a tsunami because Pushpa simply broke down at this point. She was clearly a victim of emotional abuse, something that is as damaging as physical abuse but harder to recognize and therefore confront.

Her husband had subjected Pushpa to cruel levels of criticism, which had undermined her self-esteem to such a degree that she was unable to express herself, fearing ridicule or being yelled at for doing so. She was made to feel powerless, fearful, and dependent, and her relationship seemed to erode her sense of self, self-esteem, and happiness. Emotional abuse is an insidious form of violence in a relationship.

I tenderly squeezed Pushpa's hand and told her that it wasn't her fault. Emotional abusers are great at self-deception and projecting blame onto their partners for their abusive actions, much like Kamlesh blaming his drinking on her 'disability' to provide with him a male heir. Pushpa agitatedly continued that so stressful were the pressures under which she got pregnant with her third child, that she started bleeding in her third month and had to undergo an ultrasound. What the test also brought to light was that there was a baby girl on the way. India has made gender determination tests illegal with specific intent of avoiding situations exactly like this one. The test was ostensibly only for the purpose of determining the health of the unborn child but what was less apparent is a common deviation. But as is commonly said, show an Indian a rule book and he'll either resort to corruption or find a loophole. I'm told that in India doctors will bless the couple and only tell them the child is healthy. However, on being given a healthy 'tip', they will add charmingly, but insidiously, that the proud parents should distribute ladoos—the code for a boy child, or pedas—the code for a girl child.

No pedas were distributed in Pushpa's home after the test. Just heated arguments on whether to keep the girl child or abort her. There was a hint of anger in Pushpa's voice as she brought to light that after that Kamlesh would return home every day, drunk and abusive. Ashamed in front of his friends that he was fathering yet another girl, he didn't show any regard or sensitivity towards her during the entire pregnancy. Over numerous drinking and card playing sessions, Kamlesh's friends kept harping on how expensive girls are to the family and that eventually they move away to someone else's home. They irrationally and incessantly quizzed him, tormented him, and jeered at him. The only saving grace for Pushpa through all the dramatics and insults her husband heaped on her way was the unconditional support of her in-laws. One night when Kamlesh came home and started shouting that girls grow up and go away to their 'sasural (husband's house)' and become their family, but that boys will stay and always be 'our child', Ramrati had sharply retorted, 'Kamlesh, you come home drunk and never even ask us if we've eaten roti, while our daughters, Rita, Sunita, and Gita, care for us continually and visit or call us every single day to make sure we've eaten and are fine. Who, then, in this case is "our child"?'

As I watched Pushpa compose herself and wipe her angry tears away with a handkerchief, I thought of all those countless women who must continually suffer such atrocities. Women who are tormented not just by their husbands, but by their in-laws too for not producing a boy. What of those women who endure emotional and physical abuse and have zero familial support to fight the same?

Women should not suffer in silence or be frightened. That is their undoing. They are so scared of angering their in-laws that they keep quiet, are afraid of being taken advantage of by the boss in a workplace so they don't go to work, are afraid of molestation and being raped so they amend the way they dress or perhaps even stop going out. Women can't and shouldn't live their lives in fear.

In the beginning Pushpa had been in a reminiscent state, tearful, a bit fearful, and mostly reticent. But I noticed that she was now sitting up a little more assertively, her tone had become a bit sharper, and all of a sudden her eyes flashed angrily. It excited me that Pushpa was emerging from the abyss she was in. 'We're all with you and feel deeply for what you had to endure,' I gently encouraged her to go on. She recollected how Kamlesh took his rants and outbursts to inhuman levels before suddenly submerging himself in a state of deep depression. When Kamlesh emerged from it a few days later, he sadistically would lash out at Pushpa. 'Aapke kok mein taakat nahih aiki mere liye beta paida kare.' (Your womb does not have the strength to produce a son). I was horrified. On seeing my mortified expression, Pushpa said that the family had been equally shocked and decided they would not sit quietly and watch Kamlesh repeatedly unleash his cruelty on her. It was not enough to keep pacifying him or to just insulate her and be supportive; it was time to put him in his place. Ramrati and her husband gave him a good piece of their minds and the sisters sat him down and gave him a lesson in biology. 'Before you blame Pushpa's womb for its lack of strength in producing a son for you, just know that it's the man who is responsible for either X or Y chromosomes, which determine the sex of the child. The woman only fertilizes what you send out,' they told him. And then gave him books and other resources to put all his disbeliefs to rest.

How remarkable for Pushpa to have such a wonderful family to protect her, I mused.

But then, I reminded myself that Pushpa's reality was that at the end of the day, behind closed doors, she was alone with Kamlesh. And what went on between them was a story I would probably never hear of. No matter how many times he overstepped all boundaries, no matter how much the family tried, the battle at the end of the day was Pushpa's to fight. Then again, I considered, she didn't need to look further than her own mother-in-law for direction, strength, and perspective.

Suddenly, I sat back with a sudden burst of realization. I had come here with Pushpa in mind as the heroine of my story, but in actuality, my heroine was Ramrati. Ramrati, despite her lack of education, had taken many radical steps to ensure a kind of liberalism and vision for all the women in her family. Her support of her girls highlights her celebration of birth, not gender. By allowing her children to have marriages based on love she showed her freedom from the shackles of conventions, the strength to fight such conventions. Additionally, by supporting Pushpa over Kamlesh she chose to stand up for what was right, instead of blindly supporting her own blood. Ramrati celebrates the girl child, and their rights. She is the epitome of the kind of woman that is integral to positive societal change.

Excited as I was to have discovered a powerful matriarchal figure as my story's mascot and a paragon for all to emulate, I was equally keen to know how things would turn out for Pushpa in the end. She was at a pivotal juncture in her life. Her child was dead and her husband would most certainly still want a male heir. What would Pushpa's reaction be if he asked her to bear another child? Pushpa took a long, deep breath and stated determinedly that the gender of a child could only be decided by God. 'If he so desperately wants a boy, we can adopt one and give an orphan a good life,' she said decidedly, adding that she would not bear another child. I thought of how this would please Ramrati. It must be gratifying to know that the younger women of the family will make good use all they had been empowered with and pass on the baton of progressive change to the coming generations. Because women have the power to hold the reins of change and halt it or allow the future generations to gallop forward. Nobody knows that better than Ramrati, and hats off to women like her.

Pooja Bedi is a well-known media personality. She has acted in popular films suh as *Jo Jeeta Wohi Sikandar* and *Phir Teri Kahani Yaad Aayee*, and created waves in the country with the controversial Kamasutra condom campaign which she used as a platform to promote safe sex and HIV awareness. Pooja is a relationship counsellor through her columns in *The Times of India*, *Femina*, and *Men's Health*, as well as the editor of *Timepass*, the memoirs of her late mother, Protima Bedi. She has participated in popular TV programmes such as *Jhalak Dikhlaja*, *Nach Baliye*, and many more, as well as hosted a talk show, *Just Pooja*. Pooja supports many causes, including breast cancer awareness, housing for the poor, female foeticide, maternal mortality, and child education, and has been working with charitable organizations for over a decade. She is also the chairperson of her own foundation, The Grassroots Foundation, which is dedicated to working at the grass-roots level across India.

Gopal Tanti

(Community health worker for seven years.)

Gopal Tanti belongs to a remote village called Kudabeda, in Saharapada block in the state of Orissa. She had to discontinue her studies when she was in Class 9 to take care of household chores and younger siblings. She is married to a farmer who works very hard for living, and the couple have two children, a 16-year-old daughter and a 14-year-old son, studying in Class 12 and 10 respectively. She was determined to provide education to her children, so they do not suffer the same fate as her.

In the seven years of her service as a health educator, she has successfully raised the awareness of the villagers on health care and is looked upon as a friend to rely on. She is a role model not only for the girls in her community but also boys and young men who want to change the health status of their village. She is also respected as a social activist in her village and now serves as an excellent health educator for the PU.

The Thousand-piece Jigsaw

Aditi Rao Hydari

Zulekha was hopeful for the first time in the fifteen years since she had been married and sent to Mumbai, far away from her home in Hyderabad. She held her sixth baby and waited for the cry that would signal that all was well. But this time when the rather brusque doctor spanked the baby, she gurgled and smiled, looking straight into her mother's eyes. A look that took away every little bit of exhaustion and pain from Zulekha's being.

Zulekha named her Naazma, which meant 'the one who looks after'. An apt name, for Naazma was a special child, different from all her older siblings. As she grew up her siblings spent their time beating each other up, running around, creating havoc, dressing up, hankering for things they didn't have, and almost never studying. Little Naazma, on the other hand, was content, always smiling, and looking after some creature or the other. She would pick up puppies and feed them, find homes for kittens, and she had a little bowl of grain for the few birds that were left in Mumbai. She would pick up wailing children and rock them to sleep, and she routinely and gladly helped her mother out with the housework. Naazma loved to read whatever she could lay her hands on and always had time to study. In fact, it was her dream to become a teacher.

Her classroom at home consisted of blue- and green-eyed dolls that didn't squeak any more when pressed, two toy cars that she had inherited from her brothers, one gun, and her adopted animals. She spent most of her time with them because she was much younger than her siblings and had only her mother and her cousin Yasmin, for company. The dogs would wag their tails at her furiously, looking like they were hanging on to her every word, while the cats would sit on her lap, foot, shoulder, as if claiming her and would look at her most disinterestedly as they licked themselves languidly. The birds ate copiously and shat copiously. That was one thing Naazma couldn't fathom: how could they eat and shit all at once in the same place, in her house, while she played teacher? The sparrows were okay, but the pigeons shat so much and were so noisy. But she didn't have the heart to deny them their food, shelter, and shitting space. Much to Zulekha's amusement, and sometimes exhaustion, Naazma was the local do-gooder, the Florence Nightingale. She ran her own little hospital on the street where every second day someone would arrive at their doorstep with an injured animal, which Naazma would nurse back to health with all the love and care her little being could muster.

Naazma didn't have any memory of her father. Her mother said that Sallauddin had worked in a factory on the outskirts of Bombay. He had been a loving father and husband. Zulekha told Naazma how blessed they had been because he was kind, he never beat his children, and he didn't drink. The only problem was that he was never there. From the time she came into the house as a young bride, Zulekha had managed everything on her own: the home, the children, the illnesses, and even the repair work around the house. The factory gave the workers and their families accommodation, but the factory was a terrible place to live with its toxic fumes and unsafe conditions. Vast stretches of empty, deserted land surrounded the factory, and with young girls in the house, Sallauddin insisted that Zulekha live with the children in the city, in a bustling lane where he hoped people looked out for one another. He thought they could go to school and have a better life, while he would stay at the factory and come home for a day every two weeks or so. One day when he was home, Zulekha noticed that he was looking pale. Salluaddin had malaria. He needed rest and his medicines had to be taken very precisely. He was given four days off and was to be back at work immediately after. A lot of workers had just lost their jobs and the factory was short staffed. He was lucky that the owners had retained him. Sallauddin was a good, honest worker, and the one with the longest association with the factory. He knew how badly losing his job could throw their lives into disarray, and was grateful to God that he still had his. So he went back to work after four days, but as soon as he got back, his fever returned so strongly that it weakened him far too much to work. When he didn't come home that weekend, Zulekha set off to find him. She was seven months pregnant, and struggled to make her way to the factory, catching a bus, then a train and an auto, and then having to walk for an hour. Only to learn that her Sallauddin was dead.

Naazma was born two months later. She grew up never knowing her father. Her Amma and her menagerie of animals were her life. She had heard that her Amma had a beautiful voice and sang very well, but she had never heard her sing. Naazma herself wasn't much of a singer, but she never let that stop her. She loved her mother and protected her fiercely; if anyone dared take advantage of Zulekha's kindness and generosity, little Naazma would turn into a firecracker. Her tiny face would go red, tears would well in her eyes, and she would breathe fire, much to everyone's amusement.

Naazma was 22 years when Iqbal's family moved into the house near hers. It was the beginning of the monsoon. Their family seemed very different from her own. You could tell from their Hindi that they weren't from Mumbai. They used big words and spoke in long, accented sentences, and most of the people in the slum squinted at them and scratched their heads, trying to decipher what they were saying. Iqbal and his family, in turn, took offence to the way most people spoke in their 'I have no time for you, let's get on with it' Mumbai-style Hindi. One day at the bus stop, Naazma found Iqbal coughing and spluttering angrily at someone. In true Naazma fashion, she took it upon herself to calm him down. She gave him water and explained to him that this was just how it was here. No one meant any harm. This brash way of talking was an irreparable defect in the 'Mumbaiya's' Hindi and was not to be taken as a personal insult.

A week later, an elderly man came to ask for Naazma's hand in marriage for his son—Iqbal. Naazma's sisters had been 13 when they got married; even her cousin Yasmin had not been as lucky as she. Zulekha had protected her for as long as she could, but now the time had finally come. Iqbal was an electrician and earned ₹8000 a month. It was a good and secure match. Naazma had a job too; she was teaching children at a crèche. The good thing was that once they were married they would live two houses away from her Amma, unlike Yasmin who had moved to Dubai. And perhaps Naazma would even learn to speak this very sophisticated dialect that actually sounded very beautiful. It seemed perfect, and Amma was right: how much longer could she avoid marriage? So Naazma agreed.

Iqbal had a cough on the day of the wedding. Naazma couldn't see him directly but remembered how red his face had gone in the mirror during the nikah, so very much like her's did when she was angry. It was the beginning of a new phase in her life. Iqbal seemed kind and gentle, just like how Amma described her father. She hoped they would become good friends, and that he would love and respect her Amma as much as she did. She was wondering if her niece would be allowed to come and spend the afternoons with her, when suddenly she heard the qazi ask 'Qubool?' She snapped out of her reverie and held her breath, waiting for his

Literacy Rate

India 1981–2011

Year	Population	Literacy Rate Males	Females	Gap inliteracy
1981	43.6	56.4	29.8	26.6
1991	52.2	64.1	39.3	24.8
2001	64.8	75.3	53.7	21.6
2011	74.0	82.1	65.5	16.6

Note:

1. Literacy rates for the 1981, 1991, 2001 and 2011 censuses relate to the population aged 7 years and above.
2. The 1981 Literacy rates exclude Assam where census could not be conducted. The 1991 census literacy rates exclude Jammu & Kashmir where census could not be conducted due to disturbed conditions.

reply. Iqbal replied with a cough. Three times the qazi asked and every time Iqbal responded with a cough. Naazma giggled under her dupatta; she wanted to laugh loudly, but Iqbal would have been humiliated, and after all, this wasn't a bus stop. Iqbal finally managed a loud, confident affirmative that made her smile. They were married and everything changed except the cough.

Iqbal coughed all night and all day. He barely spoke to Naazma but he was kind when he did. Iqbal was constantly ill, always cold and weak. He never brought home his ₹8000 because he hardly ever went to work. Her mother-in-law would not allow her to take him to the doctor and every hakim she brought home just made his cough worse. Naazma made him every concoction that Zulekha taught her but everything just gave him temporary relief. Finally, one day, when her mother-in-law had gone to the suburbs to visit her sister, Naazma smuggled him out to a doctor's clinic. Tests were recommended, money was spent, and they finally discovered that he had tuberculosis. It had been in his system undiagnosed for long enough to have become serious. Naazma remembered Zulekha telling her that doctors were akin to God. Iqbal's disease had been diagnosed, Allah had heard her prayers, and he was immediately put on medication. She was convinced that the medicines would cure him. After the visit to the clinic, Iqbal coughed all the way home, and she held him firmly. They had crossed the first hurdle, it would all be okay. There was something she wanted to tell him. She was pregnant, but that news could wait.

By the time Naazma told Iqbal, he was too weak to even smile at her. He died a week later. Naazma was only three months pregnant. Her in-laws moved out a month later without saying a word.

She knew nothing about them, where they had come from, where they went after that, because no one ever spoke to her in that house. They disappeared without a trace, as if they had never existed in her life.

A few months later, the landlords came and took back the house because she couldn't afford the rent any more. Naazma had to pick up her things and move back to her mother's house. Zulekha and Naazma never spoke about Iqbal or his illness or the two years she had spent with Iqbal. Naazma never shed a tear. She got back her job at the crèche, where she could work for a couple of months till the time of her delivery. Zulekha started working double shifts to support the family. Five months later Naazma delivered a healthy, happy baby boy. For the first time in her life, Naazma heard her mother sing.

Zulekha held her grandchild in her arms, tears streaming down her face, and sang to him like an angel. And the baby boy smiled and gurgled just like his mother had when Zulekha held her for the first time. From then on, every step of the way, happy or sad, their lives were filled with music. Zulekha in her beautiful voice and Naazma croaking, much to little Atif's amusement. Naazma was sure of one thing—that her son would lead a different life, that she would not let him suffer in any way, and that she would protect him and educate him and make him the best doctor in the country. At the same time she knew he could be whatever he wanted to be. A singer if he pleased. But a doctor was what she'd set her heart on. He would himself be drawn to it, she was sure of that.

Naazma had only studied till Class 8. She was brilliant in class but that came to an end when she was 13. She had come home from school to find her house uncharacteristically locked. Zulekha always left home at the same time that Naazma went to school and returned home about half an hour before her. Zulekha worked in the Sharma's house in a building down the road. They were good employers and she had worked with them for six years, so Naazma wasn't alarmed by her absence and went to her sister's house where she loved playing with her little niece. She did her homework and helped her sister make an elaborate dinner for the family. Zulekha had still not returned when the sun was melting into the sea. Naazma remembered being angry and worried at the same time. She remembered that just as she put on her school shoes to start walking towards the building, an auto stopped in front of their house and her mother stepped out of it with a plaster on her right foot and right arm.

The staircase in the Sharma's building was being washed that day, and the building society had had the lifts shut down. Zulekha had been walking behind a child who was running down the stairs. She warned the child to be careful but the child didn't pay any heed to Zulekha. Zulekha slipped trying to save him from getting hurt and slid down a whole flight of stairs. The child yelled out very loudly in fear, and people came rushing in to see what had happened. Zulekha was luckily taken to the hospital without delay. She had to be on bed rest till she healed. That day changed little Naazma's life forever. She had to take over her mother's job at the Sharmas'. Little Naazma was now the sole earner for her family.

Naazma settled into her job well while Zulekha healed slowly but never quite got back the strength in her limbs. One day, almost a year later, Zulekha decided that the strength of her body was in her will, and she was determined to get it back. If housework was too strenuous she would start a food delivery service. She would join the famous dabbawalas of Mumbai, which she did. But by this time Naazma had left school far behind her. Though she continued to read and teach herself new things in her spare time.

One day, while working at the Sharmas' house, Naazma chanced upon a 1000-piece jigsaw puzzle spread out on the children's bed. They had given up on it by the looks of it and Naazma was cleaning their room when she saw the picture on the cover of the jigsaw and the pieces strewn about. She was so distracted by the picture and the temptation of piecing it together that she put down her broom and sat on the floor to figure it out. She had almost made it to the skyline and the pillars of the Gothic structure, which looked most alien to her, when Mrs Sharma walked in. Naazma didn't notice her till Mrs Sharma leaned in to look at her work. She sprang to her feet, picked up her broom, and apologized for her transgression.

Mrs Sharma was so impressed with Naazma's skill that she asked her if she would like working with little children at the crèche in the school. She would be teaching children how to colour, do jigsaws, cut shapes, and learn their numbers. And that is how Naazma started working at the crèche in the 'big school'. She became everyone's favourite didi and was a champion solver of even the most complicated 1000-piece jigsaw puzzles. That was what she did till she married Iqbal and lost him and returned to her mother's house and had Atif.

Now she was back at the crèche but she wasn't satisfied. She was happy but something kept gnawing at her. She felt that this life didn't provide enough for Atif, and for Amma. It was her responsibility to protect them, and to make their lives better. What could she do as a mother? Atif was in those most crucial years of learning, he was absorbing everything around him like a sponge. She had seen this in the crèche too. This was a very critical time. Naazma was good, kind, cheerful, intelligent, and she had a job. But these were just basic things. Now she needed to do more, she had to take responsibility for her life, for her child's life. Nothing could be left to destiny. She wanted to give her son the freedom and the privilege to choose his own life.

When Atif turned one, Zulekha was still working with the dabbawalas, but Naazma had moved from just working in the crèche to actually teaching classes. Most of the teachers with all their degrees turned out to be far less equipped than she was, and the children in her class were always willing to learn and with great enthusiasm. But because she didn't have a degree, she couldn't get a permanent job or the full salary of a teacher.

It was then that Naazma heard of a place called Pratham, which worked with children from homes like hers. She found the address and went looking for a job, hoping that they would allow her to bring Atif with her. And that he too could begin his formal education. She thought he would have other children to play with, a clean and secure environment, one nutritious meal; how could she not dream?

But when she arrived at the address she had written down on a piece of paper, instead of Pratham, she found a garment factory. She learnt that Pratham had largely subsisted on aid from the US. But those funds had stopped coming when two aircrafts had crashed into two very important buildings. She remembered 9/11; it happened on the day that she married Iqbal. Had it been an omen? She quickly shook the thought from her mind; difficult times teach you things, and it is up to you to deal with them positively.

All that Naazma could think of was Atif, their future, her job, Amma, her salary. She worked herself to the bone, and after school she would roam the city on foot, trying to get information about job opportunities. She would walk the city in the unrelenting heat, with barely any food in her belly. She would be so tired by the time she came home to Atif and Amma that she had no energy to tell him stories, or play with him, or take him to the beach that he loved so much. It was in this state of exhaustion that she thought of Iqbal coughing himself to death. And she thought of the doctor she wanted her son to become. Perhaps she could try becoming a nurse herself. She had healed and looked after all of her animals all her childhood. It gave her a deep joy to help things get better. She remembered her mother telling her that doctors were akin to God and that they could cure any illness with their medicines. But they had not managed to save her father or her husband. And that thought brought on the doubts. What did she really know about being a nurse? She had only studied till Class 8. Sure, she was good at solving children's jigsaw puzzles and repairing their toys, but did that mean she was going to be able to help ease another person's suffering? Then she remembered how Matki, her umpteenth adopted puppy, had once needed an injection. She had gone to the chemist but he had refused to touch the puppy and helped only by shouting instructions from the far side of the shop. Matki desperately needed that injection, and despite being only a child, while listening to the chemist's panicked tirade, she managed. She gave Matki the injection, and Matki got better. The memory brought her joy and hope. Yes, nursing was just the profession for her!

But Naazma had no clue where to start or whom to ask for advice. She asked at the crèche where she taught, but no one knew a thing about nursing. But they had all heard of a place where you could learn tailoring, how to apply mehendi, and do a beauty course. The other girls in the crèche told her to not waste time with this nursing nonsense, and quickly find a skill she could pick up easily that would earn her good money. After all, they said, she had a son to raise and she was a single mother living in a crushingly expensive city. They told her about how costly nursing school was and how difficult it was to get admission because of the long waiting lists.

That evening, on the bus home, Naazma had a stroke of luck and learnt that there was a nursing college, a polytechnic, where admissions had just opened. The fees would be high, and she had no degree: that magical piece of paper which was so very important to everyone. But she decided to at least try. Naazma wasn't so young any more but she was still little; she had big, beautiful eyes and a delicate face on a slender neck and a petite frame. She stood outside the towering gates of the polytechnic, answering the gazillion questions which the guard asked her. And she stood there and she was not afraid. Finally the guard admitted to himself that this girl was tougher than she looked, and all her answers were satisfactory. So he grudgingly let her in.

She had never been to an institute like this before; it had lawns where people were sprawled, eating, studying, laughing, gossiping, putting on make-up. It was like a large canvas come alive, with so much colour and so much movement. She went into the office, and after another set of questions, was presented to an elderly woman who seemed much more relaxed than all the other people she had met on her way in. This was the principal of the polytechnic, and she told Naazma that there were fifteen hundred girls studying here and they had all finished school and that that was a compulsory prerequisite to apply to this college. Naazma was very disheartened. She knew that all colleges would have the same policy and was ready to walk out defeated, when the principal told her about the Ummeed Project. It was funded by Plan India, and would allow Naazma to send her son for Montessori education, get health care for them both, and best of all, it would provide her vocational training in nursing! The principal made a quick call, gave her the address, wished her luck, and sent her off. It was going to be possible. It was all going to work out!

The next day Naazma received news that Yasmin was back from Dubai but was not well. Naazma hadn't heard from Yasmin in a very long time, since her cousin moved to Dubai. At first, Yasmin had written to her every month, but slowly the letters became more and more infrequent and very soon alarmingly distant. Yasmin never wrote to her after Iqbal died, not once. And the only thing she sent when Atif was born was a blank card with a picture of a blue-eyed baby. Naazma, on the other hand, had continued to write. She had sent love, apologized for anything she might have done to cause Yasmin's displeasure, cracked jokes, asked after Yasmin, and asked her to share her problems with her—but it was a one-sided communication. And now Yasmin was back in Chondi, a little village by the sea near Mumbai. As soon as she heard about Yasmin and her illness, she left for Chondi. It was the same time that Zulekha left to visit her own mother in Hyderabad. Four hours, a ferry and car ride later, Naazma was in Yasmin's house, with her beautiful cousin's head on her lap. She had been too late. Yasmin was dead. They said at the house that the girl had been possessed by a demon, and the family had brought her back to India to show her to a pir baba. She went for weeks without food, she cried all the time, or she would suddenly become uncontrollably happy, laughing loudly and unable to function, or she would be picking arguments, spending money they didn't have on things they didn't need. No one understood what or why she was like this. The pir baba said he had cleansed her, but the demon triumphed and Yasmin hung herself. What had happened, how, and for how long Yasmin had suffered, Naazma would now never know.

She stayed till they buried her. She had dealt with death many times, and it was hard every time, but Atif was waiting for her and she had to be positive and look ahead. She was on her way to building a new life, a better life. She prayed for Yasmin to find peace, on her journey back on the boat. When she reached the shore she wiped her eyes, and she smiled and she set off towards her son. Atif was at the crèche, and her friend Devi had looked after him well. They had gone to the beach to play every day, there had been stories, games, and much candyfloss. The moment Atif saw Naazma he ran to her, happy, squealing, with a handful of seashells dripping with wet sand. And as he bounced around her, he made her promise to bring him to the beach once a week. 'Like we used to, Amma, like we used to.' Naazma couldn't remember the last time she had seen Atif look at her that way. He was thrilled, jumping and laughing, and so full of life. The realization hit her like a ton of bricks. Atif was almost three, and she had become crazed in her obsession to give him the perfect life. She had been trying to live out all her dreams through her son. He was already a doctor in her eyes. She saw him now as he was: a little 3-year-old child who was happy with sweets, and trips to the beach, and tonga rides, and playing with the puppies on the street. She realized she had stopped living in the moment, in terrified anticipation of what was in store tomorrow. And she realized it wasn't worth it.

She picked her son up and made a promise to herself and to him that she would take him to the beach every week. She would take him to the zoo, that place where they show you the stars and all the other planets, music shows in the little halls in Matunga, and anywhere else he wanted to go. Atif had his whole life ahead of him. Naazma was going to start her training tomorrow with the Umeed Project and if all went well, she would hopefully be a trained nurse in a good hospital. But for the time being she was not going to lose out on life because of her fear and her obsession. This was their little world, Naazma, Atif, and Amma, and they would build it piece by piece, and there were many things to learn, and they would learn them all, together. Her little son had unknowingly held up a mirror to her. This was life, and they would make it all fit, just like that thousand-piece jigsaw puzzle.

Aditi Rao Hydari is an Indian actress who was formerly a Bharatanatyam dancer and has trained under Leela Samson since she was five. Her stint with cinema began with the Tamil movie *Sringaram.* She now lives in Mumbai and has done Sudhir Mishra's *Yeh Saali Zindagi*, Imtiaz Ali's *Rockstar,* and is currently working on the Fox and Rose movies-produced film *London Paris New York,* all in leading roles. Her mother is the renowned thumri singer Vidya Rao and her father Ahsan Hydari is a respected technocrat. Her grandfather Raja J. Rameshwar Rao is a pioneer in the publishing world. Her great-grandfather was Sir Akbar Hydari.

Seeta

(Associated with Alamb-Plan and president of Jagruti)

Seeta has four sisters and they all live with her parents. An optimist, Seeta is hard-working and a quick learner. She motivates the community to send their girl children to the school so that they can learn and lead empowered, independent lives. This year she helped to enrol twelve children in the school.

As part of the group called Jagruti, she organizes and conducts training and has helped to raised awareness of several social issues, such as child marriage and AIDS, amongst the community. For her dedicated work for the community and children's education, she has been awarded a prize by the district education officer. She is associated with Alamb-plan and is the President of Jagruti.

A Mandi Life

Namrita Bachchan

It had been another sweltering June day, the air so dry and searing it almost self-ignited. Delhi at its very hottest, offering its poorest denizens little if no respite, while the fortunate languished in chronic air conditioning. All around lay stray dogs in warm puddles, desperately seeking mercy from the infernal heat. Fruits sat rotting in wicker baskets even before they'd been sold, vegetables withered, the pavement cracked, dust rose, and flowers wilted like delicate, thin-skinned ladies unable to withstand the cruel midday assault. Cats crept stealthily into shaded crevices, old women muttered to old men who shrugged, and children were left to make the proverbial hay as the summer sun continued to shine. One and all prayed for rain.

Midnight had come and gone, and Puja lay squashed between her two sweating sisters under their mother's sagging bed in the improvised shack they called home. She was trying simply to breathe. The shallow cubbyhole was suffocatingly cramped in the summer. There was just no room. Outside, in the distance, faint hummings of a transistor radio dissolved into the night air. Someone somewhere cleared his throat and spat and, as if on cue, a train departed from the adjoining station, leaving the earth shuddering in its wake.

She swallowed sluggishly. The shaft which she occupied felt particularly cage-like and punishing on this night, a full-moon night. One meant, surely, for sharing secrets and embarking on escapades. Perhaps she could distract herself into slumber. Puja reminded herself that being snug like this was not without its merits come winter and the equally hostile cold. She ought to be grateful, really. And yet the proximity of everything seemed to be steadily closing in on her. My very own coffin, she thought.

Blood-thirsty mosquitoes buzzed around her temples, and her hair, thick and damp with perspiration, itched against her scalp. A mouse scurried across the dirt floor but she didn't dare move lest she waken one of her gently snoring sisters. She knew their unspoken fatigue. It was her own.

Ordinarily she had no trouble falling asleep. Her days were so long and laborious that despite her greatest efforts, come dinnertime she was usually nodding off over her polished thali. Wiped clean to a shine. Mother Nature, it seemed, used insomnia strictly to plague the idle rich. The poor couldn't afford to go without sleep. It was also when they dreamed.

She stared blankly across the inky darkness into the underside of her mother's threadbare mattress, inches above her nose. Hovering so close, she could smell the years of heartache, of perseverance, of stubborn hope and suffering clinging to its ancient fibres. This had been their sleeping arrangement for as long as she could remember. And she could remember everything, or so it often seemed. Her siblings counted on her powers of recollection to keep the family chronicle, and it came to her naturally. She was routinely locking things away into her memory, the good times especially. Those moments of lightness and laughter worth saving for when they'd be needed.

Her mother, a heavyset and slightly quarrelsome woman, had been unwell and immobile for eight years now. Trapped in a chain of incurable respiratory ailments, one leading inevitably to the next, her already weakened constitution worsened daily from the lack of sanitation in their environs. Slums are notorious breeding grounds for disease and theirs was no different. Every second home had a bedridden occupant. Every second week was marked by a passing.

This predicament of deteriorating health meant her mother had not actually surfaced from her bed since Puja was seven years of age, and Puja would be turning fifteen the next day. 'That's a long time to be lying flat,' her little brother would sometimes say, with that casual air of insensitivity that is the right of adolescent boys. He shared the rope-slung bed with their mother, aware of the mixed blessing, while the girls all slept on the floor directly beneath. In India, even in a poor man's home, the son is king.

Their father's untimely death many years earlier had left the family without its primary breadwinner. He had provided for his brood by sweeping the railway tracks during the day and serving masala chai on the platform at night. Being of a compassionate nature and humble disposition, he had met his end in a typically noble yet misjudged moment, when, on attempting to shoo a disoriented cow away from the tracks, he himself was subject to the fury of an oncoming train. The family grieved, but considered it a propitious demise—the cow being sacred to all Hindus. And so following months of living hand to mouth, scraping the barrel of their meagre savings, and surviving just barely on the goodwill of neighbours, relatives, and friends eager to do their bit for the kin of a karmayogi (hard working man), the sisters had begun to work. One after the other, they joined the sizeable army of young children toiling in the giant vegetable market, which circumscribed their slum—the Okhla sabzi mandi as the market was locally known, or to its insiders simply as 'The Mandi'.

'Puja...move please, so I can get up,' she heard her sister's breathless voice utter these words tight against her ear, but it made no sense since she was sitting alone at the bank of a river, the cold and clear water trickling past where she was tying the laces of her army boots. Ammu was back in Delhi. And she was here miles away as border patrol. Puja looked up at the cloudy sky, closed her eyes, and smelled the grass in a nearby field where cows grazed and a bell chimed. The oversized army tents flapped noisily in the breeze as some of the officers paced on the gravel path, crunching their heels into the stones. Her regiment had been posted in the desolate hillside landscape for just over a month and Puja was in her element settling into camp. By now she knew the drill well and carried out her duties with ease, reporting to her Major and...

'Puja, move!' came the voice again, this time snapping her out of her reverie and forcing her back to real life. 'Uff-oh, every morning it's the same story! I'm saying move and still you keep sleeping

Bravery Awards

The prime minister of India honoured twenty-three children—nine girls and fourteen boys—including two posthumously, with National Bravery Awards 2011 on Republic Day.

without consideration. I think you just pretend so you can irritate me first thing. Come on now, shift up na,' her sister Ammu prodded her and Puja giggled lazily.

'Didi, of course I don't pretend...and you also could be considerate and wait a few minutes, na? When you know I only sleep extra if I'm having my favourite dream, and this time I was posted on the border of—'

'Enough now,' Ammu cut her short. 'Chalo (Come), move so I can go fill water, otherwise again there will be none today. You know how it is in this heat, it dries up even before you can fill a bucket so everyone reaches the pump early, then when you can't wash your pretty face you'll come crying to me.'

'As if I ever come crying to you!' Puja laughed.

And so that fateful day began like any other, with nothing whatsoever out of the ordinary. Puja could never have imagined what it held in store. She rolled out from under her mother's bed, relieved to be finally stretching her sore limbs. Standing up to her full height, she tipped her head back and reached for the tarpaulin ceiling, then doubled over and touched her stubby toes before standing upright again. She rubbed her dry eyes and tried to focus.

Her brother was fast asleep on his stomach, sheltering his face in the crook of his arm, rendering him oblivious to the surrounding activity. She felt like tickling the lobe of his ear but didn't. Let him sleep, that ladla (favourite). In the corner, wedged between bed and wall, the dinky antiquated television was already switched on and her mother was watching it intently. Head raised atop a grimy, limp pillow, her mouth hung open and she was busy massaging her knee hoisted up in front of her. It was her lifeline, the television. Her connection to the wide world outside their suffocating shack and she didn't miss a minute of it. This morning she was transfixed by some saffron-robed spiritual guru, bordering on hysteria as he preached to a live audience the perils of a faithless world.

Ammu had shuffled out from under the bed behind Puja and, still grumbling, had gone to fetch water, pail in hand She was forever displeased, that one! They had yet to prepare chai so Puja brought out the cups, sugar, and jar of tea leaves, and left them on a footstool ready for Ammu's return. She touched her mother's shin lightly, then took her hand to her chest in that age-old gesture of respect before drawing aside the front curtain and loping out into the early morning sun, into air which seemed fresh and wholesome in comparison to their stuffy abode. She breathed lustily, eager to get to the mandi, where Pradnya, the eldest of the girls, would no doubt have been since dawn. She was so dutiful! Together they would diligently make their way through the bulk of garlic they'd been hired to shell. Cracking the flaky outer layers and tossing the rest to one side, over and over, mechanically, till their skin seemed to reek of it.

Each day's haul arrived in truckloads late at night. The older boys would work the graveyard shift, unloading the produce into great swells around the open warehouses and by first light the mandi's kids were already consumed by their job of peeling, separating, winnowing, and gathering the saleable goods into smaller piles. They laboured ceaselessly, come rain or shine, for they were paid not by the hour but by the kilo. The faster they worked, the more they were paid. And if they weren't fast enough, well, there were plenty to take their place.

Puja hurried down the narrow lane, plaiting her wet hair as she ducked past lines of heaped washing and tangled wires. She turned the corner of their waking slum and stepped straight into the systematic bedlam that was the mandi morning. Sheeesh! The first thing to accost her was neither the sight nor the sound, but always the smell; that overwhelming pungent stench of rotting vegetables which pervaded the air, given the mandi's dumping ground lay directly parallel to the open market. She doubted she would ever grow accustomed to it. Yet within seconds she was no longer holding her breath.

She cut a path down the centre, as she did every single day, towers of precariously stacked crates to either side of her. They made a colourful backdrop to the chaotic activity taking place below. Men and women scurrying this way and that, hollering at the top of their lungs as human chains converged around mountains of green. Children propelled rubber tyres along with sticks and got in the way of everyone including the stray goats that wandered aimlessly around, wanting naturally to be a part of the action. The route to her spot on the far side of the sprawling armory was so familiar that Puja could have traced it blindfolded. She strode past a low, deep wall of pale red tomatoes and, sticking her hand out quickly, plucked one; she hadn't had time for breakfast. Not even for tea. Distractedly she ate the flesh whilst dodging cartloads of fresh cauliflower ready for the morning sale. From the corner of her eye she spotted Bittoo, the Nepali boy, and his pallid friend whose name she could never recall. Why was he always so shy? Hiding behind Bittoo like a village bride. No wonder the caustic mandi bullies made fun of them, dubbing the duo guru aur chela (teacher and student).

She herself was not the taunting kind. Never did Puja rag the newcomers; in fact they seemed to gravitate towards her, sensing her inclination to shield them. Very often she could be found with a long trail of little ones tailing her eagerly, as though she were a teenage Pied Piper, and the mandi a kind of Hamelin. She had grown up in this market. No part of it jarred on her. Not the boorish merchants nor the flagrant buyers, creating a ruckus every day over bargains. Being predominantly male and often belligerent, the mandi provoked most of the young girls to behave like nervous sheep, herding together in awareness of their vulnerability in those surroundings. But Puja was different. Assertive and self-assured, she was confident nobody would harm her and so nobody did. It helped that she was well-built—short, but stout and sure-footed. It was her spirit which was her true protector, however. Unlike Archana, whom she could see now squatting over a pile of parched shavings flailing about for lost garlic, Puja was not delicate.

'Achha, so you decided to take half-day?' Archana teased.

The two had been inseparable since childhood. It was one of those friendships which seemed to be the inheritance of a past life. Good karma carried over. Puja sat next to her and began to work, her hands taking to the task almost as a natural reflex of being in that environment. She signalled to her sister to take a break now, head home for a quick tea if she wished, but Pradnya didn't budge. She was a tireless worker, serious and reserved. Being the eldest of the four children Pradnya had been forced to grow up the quickest, following their father's death and their mother's decline. Archana on the other hand chatted genially, bringing Puja up to date on every little thing which had transpired in the hours since they'd parted. Apparently, and quite covertly, she had received an anonymous love letter and the two were in a frenzy of guesswork as to her Romeo's identity. Giggling and blushing, on and on did they go. The hours passed in the usual repetitive fashion. Till just short of noon, when she heard the first distant yelp. That first unnerving sound of a being in agony. At the outset it was possible to mistake the source for an afflicted dog, which is what she did. The mandi attracted all sorts of dejected animals and sadly it was not uncommon to witness them being hunted away with a stick by some especially coarse barnyard brute. She never did like the idea, but Puja carried on working anyway.

It was when she heard the same pained yelp for a second time that Puja knew it had emanated from a child, and there was no question of ignoring it. The mandi was as loud and throbbing as ever but somehow the distant cry had managed to filter past all the commotion and find its way to her. A fleeting moment of misgiving seized her and then Puja knew she must act without delay. On her feet already, Puja began walking, at first distractedly, trying to locate the whereabouts of the sound, then a little faster till she was trotting past the outer wall, past the parked trucks and oceans of produce, past the labourers on their midday smoke breaks and running towards that wailing sound. Somebody is in serious need of help, she thought in alarm, quickening her pace even more. The wailing had turned into a low, tortured moan and it was making her empty stomach lurch. She knew she was close. Archana, panic-stricken, followed like a loyal puppy, asking, 'What is it? Wait! Where are you going, Puja? Wait...'

Puja veered in the direction of the sound, heart racing and palms clammy with sweat, dreading what she might find. In retrospect she could not have explained her sense of urgency, this primordial need to respond to the cry, but at that moment her instinct was guiding her and Puja took heed of it. She would always be grateful she did.

Some time later, they found themselves scattered around a drab, empty plot of land lying at the back of an Okhla clinic. Puja, Archana, Pradnya, Ammu, Archana's older brothers, the two Nepali boys Bittoo and Bijuli—they had finally learnt his name—and a dozen other children of varying ages from the mandi. A lull had settled over them as in the hour after a dust storm. The youngest members of the group fiddled restlessly while the girls murmured, but Puja was uncharacteristically still. The force of the day had temporarily snatched the bounce out of her and she was going over its events in her head, gravely.

The scene which had awaited her at the end of her frenzied flight was one she would never forget. After all, wherever in the world you may live, it isn't every day you encounter a little boy beaten ruthlessly.

He was lying in a trembling heap, curled in on himself, face bloodied and clothes torn; his shoulder had been dislocated and hung at an unnatural and sickening angle. The whole sight was pitiful, the ugliness of it amplified by his anguished wailing broken only by fits of blood-flecked coughing. Puja knelt down and took him ever so gently in her arms. When he opened his swollen eyes slightly she recognized him as her young friend Sachin. A sweet little boy just shy of nine, the son of a single mother from her stretch of the slum. He cried achingly, surrendering himself to her embrace, and her face burned. Who could have done such a thing? She felt the shreds of his bloodied shirt against her pounding chest as he lay crumpled in her lap. She had to get this poor child to a doctor. Now.

Meanwhile Archana too had arrived on the scene. The colour had drained from her face and she was trying very hard not to cry. Puja saw her and said, 'We have to do this together, okay? Just have faith in God.'

Archana nodded, her voice small but resolute, 'Of course, Puja.'

With the utmost care Puja began shifting Sachin into Archana's arms; she knew from a first-aid television programme that the badly injured ought to be kept still. She did not want to unknowingly make things worse. He was convulsing in agony but Sachin allowed himself to be moved, his wailing softening to a muffle, and Archana cradled him tenderly.

'I'm going to call for help, you'll manage, na? I'll come back as soon as I can, promise, you just keep him like this,' Puja said, untying her dupatta as she stood up and covering Sachin with it gingerly. 'It's okay, Sach, don't be scared. We're with you, everything will be okay.'

And with that she turned on her heel and started running, as fast as her eager legs would carry her, past everything and in the direction of the only phone she knew.

'Dada!' she almost bellowed, folded over and out of breath, 'Give me your mobile!'

Puja glanced upwards, hands on her knees as she gasped for air, and saw him giving her a quizzical look. 'Dada it's an emergency, I need your mobile now!' she huffed. Puja was aware of the authority in her voice but could not contain it. Never had she spoken that way to the avuncular merchant who had employed her since the age of ten. And yet on his part he had known her long enough to trust that if she were imploring him in that manner, there must be a reason for it. He obliged, handing her his mobile phone and Puja immediately punched in the digits 1098 followed by the green button, and waited for the call to connect. She gripped the phone against her ear as she tried to catch her breath. It was a helpline number the locals had been provided with for medical emergencies and she had seen it painted on the slum walls here and there. The phone rang at length before someone at the other end finally picked up. After an excruciating few minutes of speaking to one dispassionate person and then another, of being put on hold and passed around, of repeating her case over and over, Puja was typically told to wait. To sit and wait for a little while till a pickup van was available, at which point it would be sent to her area of the mandi to help with this injured child whom she had called about. That was all they could say for now. There was a waiting list for those in need of assistance and she was on it.

Frustrated, she disconnected the phone and held it out to her concerned employer who had overheard her end of the futile conversation. 'They said I should wait,' she said dejectedly, 'Someone will come...'

'Where is Sachin?' he asked.

'With Archana near the back gate, I left them there together, Dada, and I have to get back. He's bleeding very badly,' she replied, her voice tense.

'Then you can't wait, beta, you have to go now. There's a clinic at the end of the main road,' he offered, 'where you turn for the Hanuman Mandir, right next to the dispensary. It will be quite a long trek but if it's as serious as you say, it may be the only thing to do. Catch hold of someone to carry him.'

She thought for a minute but knew he was right; there was no sense in waiting. In India everything took its own sweet time. Puja suddenly had an idea. What if she used a handcart? It would be so much faster than trying to transport the boy there on foot. 'Dada, I have a favour to ask...' she started. He tried to imagine where this was going. 'What if I use one of your carts? It would be much easier to push him on wheels. I'll ask the others to help. Please, Dada, he's small and light…and it might save his life.' She looked at him beseechingly and he found himself shaking his head 'Okay, beta…yes.'

Puja got to work immediately, with the help of her sister Pradnya and a few other children who had been standing around observing inquisitively. In no time they had cleared one of the loaded carts, dumping the garlic quickly back onto the floor and covering it with sacks. She was about to start pushing it when she turned and put her hand out to touch Pradnya. 'Didi,' she said, 'please will you find Sachin's mother. She needs to know.'

Pradnya looked at her admiringly; she seemed like such a responsible adult at this moment, thinking of everyone and everything. It was hard to imagine Puja was just her kid sister.

'I'll find her and meet you there,' she said reassuringly. 'Go carefully.'

And so Puja with the help of a gaggle of mandi adolescents began steering the handcart out of the warehouse and into the open. The exercise proved to be more difficult than she'd imagined, with the cart jogging vigorously and the litter strewn everywhere adding to the already uneven surface of the surrounding grounds. They turned the corner to where the delivery trucks were parked and rattled the cart along the boundary wall of the mandi, trying to make haste without it toppling over. A few of them were ardently pushing the cart beside Puja while a few others were running alongside it, calling out words of encouragement. All of a sudden and without any warning whatsoever, two pairs of hands, stronger and more assured, appeared to stabilize the empty cart with their grip, taking charge of it from Puja. She for paused a moment and to her great surprise recognized her helpers as the two Nepali boys, the ones whom everyone liked to mock. Word was spreading in the mandi, and they had been the first to abandon their posts so they could be of help. A lump rose in her throat.

When she arrived at the spot, they were exactly as she'd left them. Archana had become bleary-eyed from sitting in the afternoon sun but was still holding Sachin who was breathing but had otherwise lost consciousness. After the initial expressions of shock and horror, the kids organized themselves to get the job done. A few of them held the wheels steady while the Nepali boys raised Sachin carefully out of Archana's lap and placed him onto the hard surface of the cart.

It was never going to be easy navigating a vegetable handcart carrying an injured child through main-road traffic but the group was sizeable so people miraculously made way. The Nepali boys were lean but had stamina and never once let up. They steered the cart as carefully as possible away from the larger stones and ditches, covering ground steadily along the way. Puja was so grateful for their presence. As they approached the Hanuman Mandir, which she had been directed to keep to her left, Puja said a silent prayer for Sachin. She had no doubt all the others did the same. She spotted a signboard with a green cross a few yards down and knew it must be the symbol of a medical dispensary. They had found the clinic at last! She hurried ahead.

'My friend is outside, Sister, he's very badly hurt! Please attend to him. We brought him as fast as we could!' Puja said emphatically. The clinic was tired and poky but smelled acutely of disinfectant, which was somehow reassuring.

The nurse on duty looked up at Puja then followed her outside to where the others had gathered. She checked quickly to see if Sachin was breathing, reaching out to take his pulse, and sighed, saying, 'Lord have mercy, this child needs immediate attention. Please step aside, we will take him from here.' She picked him up off the cart with the help of one of the orderlies and carried him briskly inside. The children were left assembled around the bloodstained cart.

A few minutes passed and the nurse returned. She took a deep breath and said to Puja 'Where are the boy's parents? He's quite serious. Doctorsahib is with him.'

Puja informed her that his mother should be arriving shortly.

'We will require an advance payment for the treatment,' the nurse said apologetically. 'Please understand, it's our policy. Without some kind of advance we cannot treat the patient. This is a private clinic, not a charity.'

Puja looked at her aghast. She had learnt that Sachin had been beaten for stealing potatoes. He had been mumbling incoherently before losing consciousness and had uttered words to that effect, lying in Archana's lap. If that were the case, how on earth would his mother cover the medical bill? She could not even afford to give him food! And here they all were, his friends, gathered together with empty pockets.

Someone behind her stepped forward; it was Bittoo, the more vocal of the Nepali boys. He reached across and handed the nurse a fistful of notes saying, 'Take this as advance, it's more than enough, Sister, the rest we'll pay later.'

The nurse clutched the stash in her hand and went inside.

Puja gathered her wits about her and stood up to go, feet aching in the haggard chappals. The day had all but depleted her, but Puja had so much more to do. She spoke quietly to Archana, 'I'm going back to the mandi for a bit, there's something I have to do. Didi will be reaching with Sachin's mother; you stay here and wait for them, okay? I'll come back as soon as I'm done. In any case you're not alone.' She motioned to the others hanging around. 'Try to drink water meantime, okay? Chalo, be strong, I'm just coming.'

By the time she returned to the mandi news of what had happened was everywhere. Everyone, or so it seemed, was gossiping about it. That in itself was reassuring, mused Puja, that you couldn't beat a child to a pulp and expect it to go unnoticed. She had decided to raise the money for Sachin's medical expenses by enlisting the help of the mandi's youth, urging them all to chip in. It was the only way out that Puja could see. She started with her corner of the market and steadily made her way around. To each and every child, adolescent and teenager, she said the same thing: how they all had to stick together and stand up for each other, that if tomorrow, God forbid, it were one of them in trouble they could also expect the same. She was earnest and persuasive, collecting the money in her bloodstained dupatta as she progressed. Almost every young person in the mandi made a contribution, down to the very youngest, giving whatever they could spare. They recognized the need of the hour, and they rose to meet it. Back at the clinic Puja counted it all out, dividing the notes from the change, and was heartened to find she had raised ample funds to cover the costs. Unless of course something unexpected came up. They had been given little indication of Sachin's condition and were waiting anxiously to hear from the nurse.

She was still lost in thought when the first drops fell. Puja had been sitting apart, staring down at her feet, thinking about Sachin and the events of the day. A gentle child, Sachin had grown up without a father and had faced his share of hardships because of it. Puja hoped dearly he would survive. Nobody deserved to die for being hungry. The handcart stood wistfully to one side of the empty plot, the odd raindrop making a tapping noise upon hitting its wooden surface. Her two sisters had bought a few bread buns and were distributing them quietly to the children who hadn't eaten for hours, but nobody had much thought for food so they nibbled half-heartedly. Nearby, the traffic slowed, birds called out to each other feverishly as the last of the evening light lost out to the drizzling darkness. They continued to wait.

At long last, the clinic door creaked open and a willowy form floated out of it. Sachin's mother had an unusually calm air about her and the gathering braced itself for the news. She came up to where Puja was seated and, placing a hand on Puja's own, she turned to face the others. 'Sachin will never be able to repay you for what you did today,' she said humbly, 'but please accept my blessings from his side.' With those words she turned and went back inside. They all understood. He was going to be fine.

In the months that followed, everyone noticed a change. Not a dramatic, outward change that took place overnight, but a subtle and pervasive shift which was gradually altering the way the mandi's youth felt about themselves, and how they could expect to be treated. In standing united they had been able to fend for themselves, and this freed them from being wholly dependent on the elders. It also meant they had shamed the mandi into taking advantage of them a little less. For whatever reason, whether fear or something else, Sachin had never revealed the identity of his aggressor. Still, it was clear that he had been battered that day by an adult. And though the younger members of the mandi continued, on occasion, to get slapped around, they had shown with their solidarity that physical abuse was not something they were willing to tolerate.

In addition to the implicit changes, the outreach programme working with the slum's children had also become increasingly active since the incident. They had been especially impressed with Puja for her handling of the crisis and made an example out of her for the local kids to follow. She was appointed leader of her area's contact group and the counsellors made a special effort to engage her in their classes. It was evident she possessed the kind of potential that deserved a chance outside the mandi, and they hoped to find a way of bringing it to fruition.

Weeks passed, and with January came the worst of Delhi's winter, but also Republic Day. Puja had been told that as part of the year's festivities their NGO initiative would be conferring her with a special award for what they deemed to be her bravery. Though thrilled to be felicitated on a patriotic day, she was also slightly embarrassed as she had never really looked upon what she had done as heroic; she truly saw it as the duty of a friend. Nevertheless, she allowed herself to get excited as the day drew near, waking up on the twenty-sixth morning shivering with cold in her moth-eaten blanket but warmed in her heart by the anticipation of her coming moment.

She dressed self-consciously, wanting to look nice, and headed out with the others to the maidan to watch the proceedings. The makeshift stage had been done up elaborately in the Indian tricolours, and everywhere paper flags flapped animatedly. Troupes of children decked out in creative costumes danced and sang giddily to blaring music, putting on practised performances for all in attendance. It was a big national holiday and even the mandi celebrated it with pride, though the truth was that little had changed for them since Independence. Everyone was in high spirits, celebrating with total abandon, especially Puja who was surrounded by family and friends. Her siblings were hardly able to keep the pride from their faces. The highlight of the event by far was the presence of a pair of television soap stars seated on the stage as special guests. The organizers had roped them in as goodwill ambassadors and they seemed genuinely happy to be there in support, smiling broadly and lapping up the adulation.

Her name was announced, and Puja stood up grinning from ear to ear; her moment had come and the crowd cheered. Someone on a microphone was saying something about her but Puja wasn't listening; she was lost in the euphoria. She walked up on to the stage and shook hands with everyone shyly before accepting her little trophy. Then she stood still for a minute, facing the crowd, taking in the scene before her as she caught sight of everyone she knew. They were clapping spiritedly, just for her. She spotted Sachin smiling broadly. He was sitting next to his mother, clapping with all his might, and Puja waved to them enthusiastically. She looked around, exhilarated, and saw so many of the others too, young and old, all acknowledging her with their applause. What an incredible feeling! Puja had never felt so happy and so proud. It was only when she locked eyes with Archana who was sitting up front, beaming as she stuck her slender fingers into her mouth and whistled like a mandi boy, that Puja thought she might cry. She bit her lip and looked down. Something in that gesture, with its mixture of innocence and masti had tugged at her heartstrings just so and Puja didn't want to be caught out. She had yet to learn that being brave didn't mean you couldn't shed tears.

The night's silence was interrupted by a loud and drawn-out groan, the wooden legs of the precarious bed creaking in sympathy with her mother's aching bones. Puja blinked, transported back to the present moment, to the eve of her birthday and her restrained restlessness. She was eager for the night to pass so she might rise briskly to her own special day. Wake up and call herself fifteen.

Archana would no doubt breeze in through the draped opening that served as a front door even before breakfast. Greeting everyone in her light melodic voice and making a fuss over her best friend. She did so every year. Bringing with her some precious homemade sweets wrapped carefully in cloth and tied with fragrant flowers strung together. Her mother was a gifted cook whose skills seemed not in the least hemmed in by their humble means. This year, Puja told herself, she would share her treats with the Nepali boys. It seemed like the correct thing to do, and to hell with what the others would say!

Beside her, Pradnya sighed deeply, turning onto her back, creating a small chasm through which Puja gazed listlessly at their cluttered, compressed interiors, tracing the bluish outlines of all that was dear to them. Their home. A ramshackle collection of stools, vessels, bric-a-brac, faded garments, cups, electronics in various states of disrepair, religious paraphernalia, dabbas, carrier bags, and tired chappals jostled for space in the corners. An altar comprising a plank of wood and four mud bricks had been adjusted against one of the walls along which had been lovingly arranged an array of framed images, those of Hindu deities and Bollywood matinee idols, mostly behind panes of cracked glass.

Sharing this motley shrine were also the touching telltale signs of teenage vanity. The gilt-edged mirror with glittering bindis tacked to every corner, hairbrushes alongside a plastic tray of bobby pins, rubber bands, fancy clips and combs, gaudy bottles containing coconut hair oil and talcum powder, sticks of kohl, a matchbox, a treasured lipstick, safety pins, needle and thread, a bar of sandalwood soap, a chipped ashtray filled to the brim with junk jewellery—some earrings missing their other halves yet holding out optimistically all the same—bright pink nail polish, old scissors, bits of sponge, and of course that magic potion which is the saving grace of every dusky Indian beauty brainwashed into believing she was born the wrong shade—the all-purpose fairness cream.

Holding pride of place above all this was the year's calendar, marked prodigiously with every possible festival and public holiday. Sharing the solitary nail in the wall was a garlanded picture of Puja's father, a black and white portrait taken at some juncture of his youth which showed kind and equitable eyes. As was the custom with the deceased, one of the girls had smeared a tikka on to his forehead, and from his perch he stared benevolently back at them. His family. Watching them grow and get by.

Puja thought about the year ahead and wondered what turning fifteen would mean. She was no more a child, as her mother kept repeating. She must get serious. She knew she must continue with her weekly classes of reading and writing Hindi, home economics, which was largely about hygiene, and someday, English. These were offered for free by the local outreach programme for under-privileged children, and she had enrolled. She was a good if reluctant student, lacking academic initiative because it ate into her working hours and meant she pocketed a little less salary than she could each week. The thought pinched. Was it worth it? In a slum, every paisa counts. But Puja also knew studying was her only way to a better life. A life doing something more fulfilling than shelling garlic while daydreaming about other peoples' lives. She wanted to speak English, well. Like the glamourous stars on television whom she admired but did not idolize. And though she was undoubtedly as star-struck as the next person, her aspirations had never turned giddy or girlish. They were noble—the legacy of her father.

Her dream had always been to join the army. Ever since she was little, Puja would march around the crowded corners of their tumbledown shack, solemnly saluting. She would pronounce earnestly to whoever listened, 'I want to protect the country', imagining that the uniformed life would be well suited to her, giving her the opportunity to travel the land, serving its people, safeguarding its borders, and hoisting its flag. She wanted to earn the respect of her peers and also her nation, and knew it could never be achieved sitting on her haunches among hills of redolent vegetables—sorting, peeling, discarding.

She had a clawing hunger for knowledge, just never the bookish kind. She didn't gauge the utility of information she couldn't use. Who had the time for such things? Puja wanted to learn practical skills, survival skills, those necessary to endure the hardships of her journey ahead. Skills which would allow her to build a better home and then a better world.

These thoughts and more swirled around her head, wearing her out, and at long last Puja's eyelids slumped closed. At the threshold of elusive sleep she made a birthday pledge to the gods who listened to such things, the ones who had time for 15-year-old girls and their heartfelt wishes. In the quiet of a creeping twilight she promised to try harder. To never complain about the cumbersome two-mile walk from the mandi to the classroom. To pay attention to the volunteers who chipped in as tutors instead of fiddling restlessly on the floor mat, waiting to abscond with Archana. She decided to apply herself mind and soul to learning to speak English. How hard could it be? Half the nation had got the hang of it. Why, only last month the neighbour's son had created a buzz in their basti by gaining employment at a call centre. A call centre! Answering phones and conversing with foreigners in proper English. What a hero!

Well, she would do it too. After all, they had acknowledged her courage in the mandi, had they not? She had no reason to feel intimidated. She would learn to speak English as her first determined thrust to realizing her dream of becoming a soldier. It was about time. Once there, the world would become her oyster. Isn't that what the counsellor had said? That education opens doors? That God helps those who help themselves? Well, either way, this mandi life could not go on forever. She would have to take a chance. Claim her destiny in her own calloused hands and take advantage of the one opening that had presented itself to her, even if it came at a tangible cost. 'This time next year...' she whispered to her drifting self. This time next year she would look into their bindi-bedecked mirror and, upon finding her reflection, greet it bashfully in broken English.

Namrita Bachchan was born in Mumbai in 1976. Her initial education was in Switzerland and in England, after which she attended the Rhode Island School of Design for a Bachelors' degree in painting and art history, followed by an Associate of Arts degree in graphic design at the Parsons School of Design in New York. Her first solo exhibition, *Give Me Space*, was held at the Museum Gallery in Mumbai in November 2004. She has exhibited in New Delhi, London, Providence, and Boston as well. Namrita is also a freelance photographer, a published poet, and a book illustrator. *Deliverance*, her first volume of illustrated poetry, was released in December 2006, followed by an edition of her grandfather Harivansh Rai Bachchan's long poem 'Madhushala—The House of Wine' illustrated by her, which was published in 2009. She lives and works in New Delhi.

Chandu

(Kishori Prerna Manch, Tudio)

I could hardly read or write even though I had studied till Class 5. That day at the camp the teacher insisted that I show her something I could write—my name, the village's name, the name of the school I had studied at. When she saw what I had written she said, 'This girl will not be able to study any further.'

I will complete my BA then I am sure I will get into BEd. After which I plan to do MA and MEd. Then I will study for the civil service exams and try to get into IAS. And I am sure I will…I know I will.

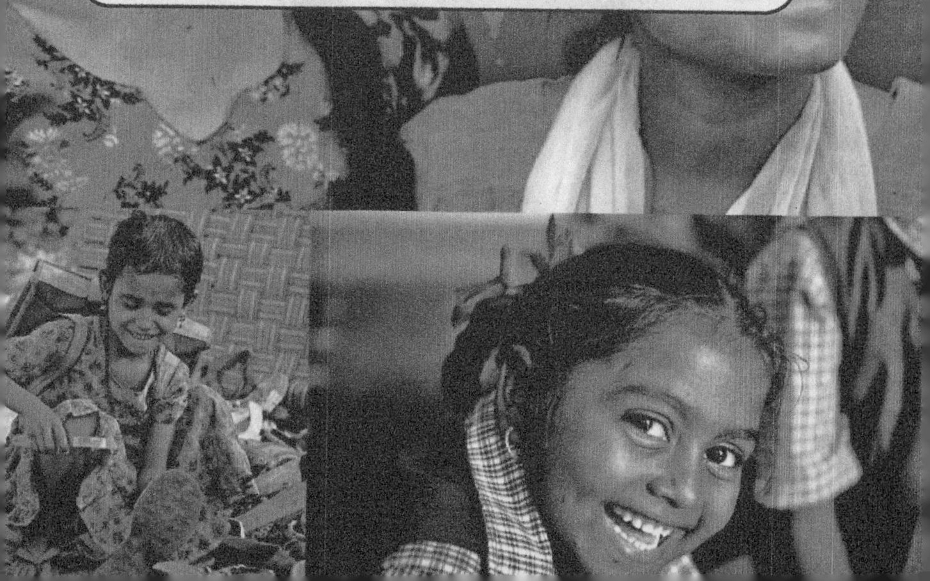

Dignity

Nafisa Ali Sodhi

The Brahmaputra is a mighty, ever expanding river, and every year the monsoon plays havoc with it, causing it to swell and spill out, breaking banks and swallowing the surrounding low-lying area. This yearly phenomenon wreaks devastation for months, uprooting thousands of farmers from their lands, rendering them homeless. And there is very little people can do when face to face with the brutal and naked force of nature. Gul Afshaan is a lifetime away from her home in Assam. She and her family are one of the victims of such floods. They lost everything, and were left homeless, destitute, and without a chance of survival, the government doing nothing to bail out such survivors. If it hadn't been for their chacha (paternal uncle) in Delhi, who, out of his good grace, called them to come and live with him, they would have a tough chance of just surviving.

She greets me in Hindi, and I am taken aback by her fluency with the language.

'When did you learn to speak in Hindi?' I ask her.

'It was only after we came to Delhi that I learnt to speak in Hindi. I tell my father that my Hindi is not good,' she replies shyly.

'No, your Hindi is very good,' I assure her.

Gul Afshaan and her family arrived in Delhi, weary and penniless, and found themselves a home in Khatta slum in the Sarai Kale Khan area next to the Nizamuddin railway station. They don't own the juggi they live in and continually fear being moved by the government authorities. The first few years for the family in Delhi were disorienting, alien, and involved back-breaking work just so they could keep their heads above water. Soon they found their way around, and started working as ragpickers in the city. They pick through the various garbage sites and sell the bottles they find to the kabadiwalas. They have been doing it for the last nine years. Young Gul Afshaan also helps them by getting plastic bottles from the nearby police station.

When I look at 13-year-old Gul Afshaan I see a gleam in her eyes. A hunger to learn, and a grit which takes me some time to get accustomed to.

She tells me her story. Gul Afshaan started attending classes at the Contact Point run by the NGO Chetna from 3 to 5:30 pm a year ago. Her mother's initial reaction was one of natural scepticism as they had already been through a lot in life. She was wary of the activities being held at Contact Point, and didn't see how an education would help them to alleviate their dismal condition. She would not allow

Women Ragpickers

There are an estimated 15 lakh men and women who eke out a living by rummaging through garbage and landfill sites looking for material they can sell to small, unorganized scrap dealers who then recycle them. As they are unorganized, their main complaint is that authorities often bar them from landfill sites and garbage collection areas, which for them means a loss of income and livelihood.

The ragpickers' associations from seventeen cities across India have now formed an 'alliance' in Pune. Towards the end of January, about 200 ragpickers from the Alliance of Indian Wastepickers (AIW) gathered near Ahmedabad for the first national conference. Union Environment Minister Jairam Ramesh was the chief guest, to whom they submitted a memorandum asking for recognition.

her daughter to visit the organization. However, the workers at Chetna persuaded Gul Afshaan's mother and emphasized the importance of a girl child's education, and she finally relented.

Gul Afshaan took to the organization like a fish to water. She made rapid progress and in no time she became a very active participant and group leader. Like any other child her age, Gul Afshaan loved playing games like skipping and playing ball at the Centre and looked forward to her interaction with the other children.

'What did you do with the organization?' I ask her.

'We had a lot of fun,' she says, her eyes lighting up. 'We studied, played, and learnt about our rights. We also learnt how to dance and paint, and we acted in plays. There were many melas (fests) and competitions in which we had to participate. Once we also visited the zoo, which was very exciting.'

When her mother saw the changes in Gul Afshaan's personality after attending classes at Contact Point, her suspicion turned to joy. Her parents were so happy to see their daughter enjoying new skills and doing well at school that they also sent their other four children to Contact Point.

After attending the classes, Gul Afshaan has become more confident. Her enthusiastic disposition soon led her to outgrow Contact Point, and since the beginning of this year she has joined the local government-run school, which the organization helped her gain admission to. She has grown up to be a good organizer. She is a bright student, a helpful classmate.

The story, however, is not all roses for Gul Afshaan. Life has dealt this young fifth grader a tough set of cards. Her real life starts when her school hours draw to an end. During the rest of the day our formidable Gul Afshaan works as a ragpicker. Over the years she and her family have managed to make a pact with the local police. When they go picking plastic bottles at the station, she prefers to have a dialogue with the policemen where she tries to convince him to let them collect bottles, rather than go about it like a petty thief. 'Even we need to make money to eat so please do not stop us from coming here,' she reasons with them.

I ask her if she fears that the police might ever resort to violence. But she is smarter than her years, and is aware that the police have no right to hit children. 'If ever they do, we can call on the helpline 1098,' she tells me in that tiny voice of hers. In the presence of the more senior officials they do not enter the station because she says, 'Even the policeman has to work to survive and feed his family, why get him into trouble.' They go back to the station only after the senior officials have left.

I ask her how much they earn by ragpicking to which she answers, 'These days I go to the station only at four o' clock in the morning and am back by 6:30 am as I have to attend school. Papa makes ₹2000 a month. He picks garbage in a pushcart, going from one colony to another. And I make about ₹100, on a good day.'

'That is good, honest work,' I tell her. 'He is helping to keep the city of Delhi clean.'

'Yes, we are poor so we have to work to survive,' she says.

'Everyone has to work to survive, not just poor people. And your father is doing good work. One is rich and poor based on what is in one's heart and mind, right? You will find many people in jail who have crores of rupees because they wanted still more money.'

She agrees to this. 'Yes, one should be honest. My father is poor but he is an honest man.'

Gul Afshaan gives all the money she earns to her mother but occasionally asks to keep some for herself. She loves to buy and eat fruits with that money. 'Why eat silly things, when it is fruits that make our blood and give us strength.'

I am curious about this little girl and wonder what she is going to do about her education.

She tells me, 'I want to study and then my parents will get me married.'

'But you must continue to work so that you can be economically independent,' I say to her.

She is quiet for a moment and then says, 'Yes, I would like to be, but my parents are keen to get me married.'

It is such a waste. I can understand her parent's dilemma. A girl in India is always considered a liability, and her sole purpose seems to be to help around the house, then be married off and help around her in-laws' house. Financial independence is something which is very rarely considered a possibility. I worry about Gul Afshaan, for here is a child who has the potential to make so much of herself rather than just be someone's wife or daughter.

'If you work, save money in a bank account, it will be good because then no one can say anything to you as you will be strong and independent. Do your parents have a bank account?' I ask.

'Yes, my father has a joint account but the other person withdrew all his money and ran away. I do not know the details, but my parents were very upset when he took all of my father's savings.'

'That's why you should have joint accounts only with a person you can trust. It's always better and smarter to have an independent account.'

'Yes, one should never have a joint account. I will tell my father this. He is so upset that he does not want to put money in the bank any more.'

Gul Afshaan spends half the day with her siblings on their own. In a city like Delhi where child abuse is rampant, I wonder if she knows the risks involved in her roaming about the city unattended, and ask her, 'Are you aware that children can be sold and abused?'

She is a smarter cookie than I expected. 'My brother was abused by our neighbour. Our neighbour once tempted him into his room with some sweets. My brother later told my father, who had a big fight with the neighbour and threw him out of the slum. Ever since that incident all of us have become very careful. One has to be alert all the time or else somebody can take advantage of you.'

There is little that this young girl isn't aware of. She's tough and confident, and has an unnatural air of maturity for her age. I think of other, more privileged children her age, and wonder at how most of us take our freedom and security for granted. She is miles away from her home, living in challenging conditions, yet her outlook is indefatigable. I wonder about their fate, what life has in store for Gul Afshaan and her family. Will another calamity, like the flood which caused their exodus, force them out to different pastures, where they will have to relearn and reconstruct their life from scratch?

'Do you miss your village? The weather is better there. Delhi allows you to earn but the expenses are also more than in the village, right?'

She answers my question with a simple sentence. 'I would like to stay here now. I know this place.'

And I know that she is here to stay.

Nafisa Ali Sodhi was born in 1957 to renowned photographer Ahmed Ali. She made an entry into the Indian fashion arena by winning the Miss India 1976 pageant and later was adjudged Miss Internationals Runner-up in 1977 in Tokyo. She also made a distinct entry into the Indian film industry by being a part of movies like *Junoon*, *Major Sahab*, *Life in a Metro*, and a Malayalam film *Big B*.

She is an eminent social worker, with her crusade on HIV/AIDS being recognized globally. She started a Care Home—Ashraya—for people infected and affected with HIV/AIDS and cares for tuberculosis-infected patients through the government-sponsored DOTS programme. She was also the official government delegate for India at the Forty-ninth UN Summit on 'The Status of Women' held in New York in March 2005.

A Note on Plan

Plan in India is part of Plan International, one of the world's oldest and largest children's development organizations. Founded more than seventy years ago, Plan has no political or religious agendas. Plan works at the grassroots level in 48 developing countries to empower communities to overcome poverty so that children have the opportunity to reach their full potential—and children are encouraged to be actively involved in the process. Plan unites, empowers, and inspires people around the globe to champion every child's right to survival, develop to the fullest, be protected and participate fully in family, cultural and social life.

Plan India is a nationally registered child centered community development organization. For over thirty years, Plan and its partners have been helping communities throughout India to help themselves, so that children have access to their rights including the right to protection, basic education, proper healthcare, a healthy environment, livelihood opportunities, and participation in decisions which affect their lives. Plan India currently works in nine states in India and has impacted the lives of over a million children across 5000 communities. Plan India is implementing 247 thematic projects and 15 advocacy projects through 100+ partner organizations.

Because I am a Girl

Because I am a Girl is a campaign launched by Plan to promote girls' rights and lift millions of them out of poverty. Across the world, girls face discrimination because of their gender and age, and this leaves them at the bottom of the social ladder. For example, research has shown that girls are more likely to suffer from malnutrition; be forced into an early marriage; be subjected to violence or intimidation; be trafficked, sold or coerced into the sex trade; or become infected with HIV.

The Because I am a Girl campaign is geared towards equipping, enabling and engaging girls of allages to aquire the assets, skills and knowledge necessary to succeed in life. Plan is attempting to initiate a change at a number of levels (i.e. local, national, international) with the assistance of a number of partners.